SELF-HELP BOOKS STINK

Why can't women stop resorting to all those stupid self-help books that ultimately ruin perfectly good relationships? Why can't the people who write those don't-worry-I-can-manage-your-problems-since-you're-too-insecure-and-inept-to books mind their own business and let us live our own lives? I'm sick of all those bestsellers that make men feel about as appealing as road kill on the freeway. I'm sick of having every female problem from PMS to static cling blamed on us Normal Men. And I'm sick and tired of women thinking they're the only ones who get to be misunderstood.

It's time we men spoke out—hey, we got our friggin' feelings, too, you know. So to all those stupid self-help books out there in all those stores and shopping malls, I say, with raw unvarnished male abandon: *Make my day!*

NORMAL MEN/ DESPERATE WOMEN

or

**Men Who Love Women
Whom Women Don't Like Much
Since Women Think
All Men Are Jerks**

or

**Men Who Love Women
Whom Women Don't Care For
Because They Hate Men
Who Think They Love Them
But Don't Really Have Any Idea
Of What It Is They Love**

*The Self-Help Book for Men
Who Are Tired of Being Dumped On by
Women Who Can't Get It Together*

TRIPP EVANS

ST. MARTIN'S PAPERBACKS

NORMAL MEN, DESPERATE WOMEN

Copyright © 1989 by Tripp Evans.

Cover art by The Dynamic Duo.

Library of Congress Catalog Card Number: 89-70258

ISBN: 0-312-92486-0

Printed in the United States of America

St. Martin's Press trade paperbacks edition published 1989
St. Martin's Paperbacks edition/March 1991

10 9 8 7 6 5 4 3 2 1

To my Beta wife,
without whose Alpha diligence and
Gamma understanding this book
would never have been completed

CONTENTS

Introduction   1

Male Profile Questionnaire   24

Female Profile Questionnaire   29

PART I: Getting To Know Thyself   35

PART II: Women—Can't Live
    With Them . . .   61

PART III: Coupling Couples   105

PART IV: Can My Type Be Edited?   149

Conclusion   177

Tests, Quizzes, Interrogations,
    Examinations, and Probes   187

INTRODUCTION

Look! Up in the sky! It's a bird, it's a plane, it's DESPERATE WOMAN!

Yes, Desperate Woman, who, disguised as the the efficient, resourceful, and frustrated woman of the Eighties, fights a never-ending battle for ownership and control of a man, any man, any NORMAL MAN!

And who's that Normal Man? It's you, and you, and, yes, you—yeah, even you, the guy picking his nose over there in the corner. The Normal Man is any man in a relationship with a woman; any man who doesn't want his wife bugging him about taking out the garbage when he's watching the big game; any man who feels like drinking with the guys without a girlfriend getting all pissed off because he forgot they'd planned some stupid date at her parents';

any man who wants to get through these times of global deforestation, eroding ozone layers, threats of nuclear holocaust, and trillion-dollar deficits without wasting time playing the how-to-find-the-mate-who's-right-for-you game.

Who exactly is Desperate Woman? She's any woman sixteen and older. (Note: Training starts in infancy.) She's frantic to find a man who will go out with her, marry her, give her children, money, real estate, and more. Yet she has the nerve to be particular. Desperation won't keep her from busting your nuts about practically everything, such as your meager salary, your stupid friends, your slumped shoulders. Not very pretty, is it?

How do you know if you're in a relationship with a Desperate Woman? (Take my word for it, the chances are upwards of 96.2 percent.) Answer the following questions with a simple yes or no:

1) Is she constantly interrupting you with stupid questions about the bank balance or your kids' drug habits while you're trying to catch the replay on *Monday Night Football*?

2) Does she call the police if you threaten to smack her mother for butting in and telling you how to run your marriage?
3) When you try to cop a feel at the bowling alley between frames, does she call you an insensitive clod?
4) When you take the time to discuss the pros and cons of Jell-O molds in a sensitive, low-key manner, does she call you a faggot if you don't agree with her?
5) Does she throw kitchen utensils at you (wooden spoons, spatulas, whisks, meat cleavers) for no apparent reason?
6) Does her behavior during "that time of the month" persist for about thirty days?
7) Do you constantly lose arguments when she somehow sneaks in disparaging references to the unimpressive size of your penis, resulting in your forgetting the brilliant point you were about to make?
8) Does she get pissy for weeks on end if you forget her birthday or your anniversary?
9) Does she completely lose it if you neglect to notice a new hairdo, outfit, weight loss, etc.?
10) Does she get pissed off if you refer, in a tone of awe and wonderment, to in-

teresting parts of other women's anatomy?

If you answered yes to *any* of the above questions, this book is for you.

Who's to blame for bringing out the worst in these Desperate Women? Who's responsible for turning all those Dr. Jekylls into Miss or Mrs. Hydes? None other than the authors of those how-to-find/use-and-abuse-a-man self-help books.

SELF-HELP BOOKS SUCK

Why can't women stop resorting to all those stupid self-help books that ultimately ruin perfectly good relationships? Why can't the people who write those don't-worry-I-can-manage-your-problems-since-you're-too-insecure-and-inept-to books mind their own business and let us live our own lives? I'm sick of all those best-sellers that make men feel about as appealing as road kill on the freeway. I'm sick of having every female problem from PMS to static cling blamed on us. I'm sick of wives whining about "giving too much" when we have to beg for a simple blow job on our birthdays.

I'm sick of women thinking they're the only ones who get to be misunderstood. I'm sick and tired of those asshole self-help–book authors making all the easy money. We men must speak out, because we men have feelings too, fuckin' A. Plus, we're bigger and stronger.

Women are always bitching that they can't find the "right" guy, or that they're constantly being attracted to the same kind of skunk. So what happens? Some dweeb decides to cash in on these women's problems and write a fast-food primer on how to find the perfect male, or at least one that's not dead yet.

All you have to do is take a look at some of the titles to realize how destructive they really are. Here are just a few of the more popular ones in a field of thirty or so on the market today: *Men Who Hate Women & The Women Who Love Them* and *How To Love A Difficult Man* (sound like how-to's for masochists); *Smart Women/Foolish Choices* (the title's a good example of an oxymoron—three guesses who the foolish choices are); *How To Find and*

Marry the Man You Want (I wonder if you find this book and *How To Love a Difficult Man* in the home fix-it and hobby sections); and *Women Who Love Too Much*—the subtitle says it all: "When You Keep Wishing and Hoping He'll Change." Think about it.

WOMAN AS CHANGE-LING

On first blush, the intent of these books is to convince women they shouldn't waste their time trying to change the characteristics, habits, or peccadillos of the men they date and/or hope to marry. Instead, these women should find someone who can make them happy and appreciate them for what they are (whatever that is). But we have a major problem: there aren't enough "good" men—heterosexual, nonhomicidal, solvent, and not hopelessly attached to their mothers—out there. And the men who do fit these criteria have a statistical advantage: more older men marry younger women than the reverse; men don't have to worry about a biological clock; and men are scared away by successful women.

The real message of these self-help books, the net, net, *net*, the bottom line—one you can only understand if you read between the lines—is, "Hurry, ladies! You don't have much time. If you can't change the man you're with, don't waste valuable man-hunting time adapting. Instead, find one you *can* change!"

Still not convinced? Below are two be-lieve-it-or-not stories from a couple of men who've been victimized by none other than the dreaded self-help–book syndrome.

Story #1

Marge and I used to have such a won-derful time together. Evenings, I'd go over to her place and sit down at the kitchen table with a brewski while she puttered around the kitchen, whipping up a deli-cious meal. I know that doesn't sound very exciting, but I sure was happy. Then, just a week ago, after a stupid argument over the M word* and how I wasn't ready to settle down yet, something weird happened. I came by after work, let myself into her apartment, and called out her name. She said she'd be right there, so I took a beer out of the fridge and sat down at the kitchen table.

Two minutes later she came marching into the kitchen—and I mean marching. You wouldn't have believed it. She was wearing some kind of military camouflage outfit, her face smeared with black and green greasepaint. A purple headband kept her pageboy in place, and she was holding a book. Well, I got to admit, seeing this miniature Rambo (Marge is five foot one) was too much, and I started to laugh. Suddenly she's screaming at me, "You pusillanimous pissant! Why don't you just stick this in your ear and rotate!" Then she threw the book in my face and stormed out the door. I ran after her and asked her what the problem was. She yelled, "You know perfectly well what the problem is!"

* M word = Marriage. If you didn't know this, you've never been in a heavy-duty relationship, you're a homo, or you're very lucky.

After that, things got kind of blurry. I think I said something like, "Aw, honey, you know I hate to see you like this." Suddenly, Marge's in my arms, sobbing away—her greasepaint smeared all over her face and looking like Alice Cooper after a four-hour concert—and saying, "Oh, I'm so happy! Let's set the date for early May! I'll call and reserve a room at Bob's Wedding and Reception Emporium first thing tomorrow! Now, you go back inside and relax while I finish my little errand. Silly me, I forgot the Velveeta for the macaroni."

I walked back into her apartment in a state of shock. It was then I picked up the book she'd thrown at me. It was one of those self-help books for women—you know, something like *Women Who Love To Make Dumb Choices When It Comes To Men When Instead They Should Take Their Lives Into Their Own Hands and Make the Men Who Hate Them Regret It*. I'm not sure. Something like that. I was really confused. What went wrong? What did I say? And what does "pusillanimous" mean, anyhow?

If you thought that was scary, check out this little scenario.

Story #2

I don't know how it happened. One minute I'm drinking kamikaze shooters with the guys down at the Blarney Stone and the next minute I'm in the basement ironing the dinner napkins—and three months have passed! I can't explain it for the life of me. When I asked Doris, my wife, how that chunk of time vanished from my life, she just laughed and said I was a real joker. I can tell you I wasn't a real joker; I was more like real upset.

Okay, okay, I didn't have amnesia or anything. I just wasn't me anymore. You know what I mean: I was me but not the me I was before I met Doris. Whatever it was that happened, it was slow and steady. It certainly caught me with my pants down.

When did I realize what was happening? Well, I was upstairs in our bedroom putting the laundry away when I found a book hidden in the back of Doris's brassier-and-sock drawer. The title was—and

I'll never forget it—*How To Change a Man You Love Into a Man You Can Live With, Because Finding a Man Who Has It All From the Start Is Like Looking For the Holy Grail With a Bag Over Your Head*. And then in smaller type right below the title it said "Men—What Do They Know Anyway?"

You can imagine how upset I was when I made that terrible discovery. What's worse, I didn't have time to wallow in my anger, because I had a casserole in the oven and the timer had just gone off. But I tell you, I got back at her. I decided then and there that I wasn't about to make her favorite dessert for dinner that night— crème brûlée with my own caramel topping—even though I'd promised.

What do the women in these two horror stories have in common? They both chose to rely on self-help books. Unfortunately, in the process they messed up two perfectly normal men.

The first case is a good illustration of the blatantly desperate woman, who appears to have exchanged a demure demeanor for that of a militant ball-buster. That, of course, was not the case. In actuality, Marge played out her little charade in order to get her boy-friend to freak out and CUD (commit under duress). She knew what she had to do to change his mind. We see all too clearly that his decision not to deal early on with the M-word thing was the wrong one.

On the other hand, the woman in the second situation is a wonderful instance of the covertly desperate woman. Realizing that her chances of finding that ideal man were virtually nonexistent, she chose to remodel her somewhat less than perfect bird-in-the-hand. The only difference between these two harpies is their style.

Change is a major hot button for the authors of these ridiculous books. Why? Because women are used to it. They're the ones who've had to adapt to change of roles (motherhood v. career girl), change of life (menopause), and change of name. Change is second nature. Unfortunately, the changes affect us guys more than we really know, and we end up paying for them one way or another.

A MAN'S BOOK

It's about time a book was written for the men in our society. It's my turn to . . . ah, help . . . help us guys deal with the women who treat this dreck as gospel. A book that addresses how women will try to control situations in order to get what they want. A book that reveals women as the insatiable manipulators they really are. A book that addresses the fundamental problem question *all* straight men face: *Why can't a woman be more like a man?*

One last point. Notice that a convenient term describes men who hate women—*misogynist*. But there's no such word for women who hate men. The closest I've found is *misanthrope*, but that's a person who hates all of mankind. Think about it, part two.

THE ANTI-SELF-HELP APPROACH

Consider this book an anti-self-help book. Instead of trying to alter the reader and show you how to "become a better person," even though you're perfectly happy as a self-centered slob, I plan to disclose just how desperate women really are and to demonstrate to all normal men that it's the women and their stupid self-help books that are to blame.

The purpose of this book is fourfold: 1) to show you where you stand, 2) to make you aware of what's being said about you behind your back, 3) to help you identify the clandestine techniques women use to change you, and 4) to expose you to the bizarre machinations of women—all women. You know what I mean?

From the obvious wielder of the rolling pin to the obsequious whines of the meek, the women of this world know what's going on in the world of relationships. And they use that information to make our lives miserable. As my father-in-law, a former C.I.A. spook, once told me, "Women are born into the world knowing everything they need to know; men are born into this world having to learn everything."

Note: This book is meant to help all men—all men in relationships with women that is. Unfortunately this primer is utterly useless to the homosexual population, though

I hate to lose that market segment. . . . Wait! I have a great idea. Okay, all you gays out there, replace all the *hers* and *shes* with *hims* and *hes*. It may take a little work, but it'll be well worth it. Or, leave them; it's up to you.

THE AUTHOR AS BATTERED VETERAN

You may have noticed—but why would you—that most of these books are written by women, victims of the very problems they claim to solve. How convenient. "Listen to me, girls, I know what you've been through. My ex-husband used to mop the floor with my head, and I figured it was all part of a healthy relationship and a clean kitchen. Imagine my surprise when I discovered that his behavior was somewhat unorthodox." Or, "Ladies, I settled for a man who forced me to eat burning charcoal briquets when I overcooked his steak. Of course, we loved each other dearly, until someone pointed out that I could have waited for the briquets to cool down a bit first. Don't make my mistake." They all make it sound like you have to suffer to sing the blues. What a bunch of manure.

I'll admit it, I've been burned a couple of times. What red-blooded American male hasn't gone out with, even married, some money-grabbing, emotion-draining, game-playing wacko? You're not normal if you haven't. At least I'm not going to cry about it, and that's the major difference between *Normal Men/Desperate Women* and all those self-help books geared to women. No sirree, not me. I'm not a victim and neither are you. They, those pesky women, have to stop playing those damn mind games, relax, and accept the dating situation for what it is: heavily biased in favor of the male. Okay, maybe the ones who dare to relax'll end up solitary old maids. Sorry, but things could be worse. Those old maids could be home-less, too. To all those stupid self-help books flooding the market, I say, as I point at my crotch with my two index fingers, "I got your victim—right here."

MY DEGREES ARE HOTTER THAN THEIRS

Most of the authors have a *Dr.* preceding their names. On closer inspection you see that *Dr.* is really a Ph.D. Big fuckin' deal—"Piled higher and Deeper" is all that stands for.

Well, guys, set your minds at ease. I'm neither a Dr. nor a Ph.D. I'm a concerned male, just like you. What are my credentials? Good question.

I don't leave home without the American Express card—my wife's if I can manage it. I'm pretty much on time with my monthly mortgage payments. I flunked out of EST. I like to read books, even ones without pictures. I hate cats. I drink tequila in a shot glass without lemon or salt. I think Morton Downey, Jr., is an asshole. I majored in psychology in college—it was the major with the fewest term papers. And writing this book is easier than working nine to five in my uncle's accounting firm.

Okay, okay, I'll answer the question. After having tabulated the results of an extensive questionnaire administered to all males with funny-sounding middle names—I'd like to thank Shere Hite for her helpful prototype—and having taught a six-week course at an accredited community college called: "Men: two heads *are* better than one," I'm ready to share my knowledge.

If I'm not going to help us guys strike back, who is?

WHY THE TITLE?

If those other books can have two or three pretentious titles, why can't I?

I chose the word *normal* because that's exactly what we men are, God damn it!

About the "desperate" part of the title, I must admit I was a bit concerned over people's reaction, but I found it came closest to summing up my feelings, was a bit punchier, and took up less space than "manipulative, schizophrenic bitches from hell."

IS THIS BOOK NECESSARY?

Is anything ever *really* necessary?

HOW IS THIS BOOK BROKEN DOWN?

This book is simple and straightforward. Well, not that simple. In order to make it worth $3.95 my publisher persuaded me to include a lot of case histories, some questionnaires, quizzes, tests, a chart or two, and some more case histories. You know, the types of stuff that helped all those other books sell. But have no fear, everything is easily spelled out.

This book is divided into four parts:

Part I: Getting to Know Thyself

Here I go into exhaustive detail about the three male personality types—Able, Baker, Charlie—bringing each to life with vivid individual profiles. Before you read these fascinating case histories, you will be asked to complete two questionnaires. The results of the first will tell you to which of the three male types you belong. The second will reveal which female type—Alpha, Beta, Gamma*—you're usually attracted to.

* I chose these terms because, let's face it, most women are Greek to us men.

You'll recognize your annoying habits, your private hang-ups, your tiresome anxieties. You'll also see how your particular category shapes and warps its relations with women. But more important, you'll learn how to live with your habits and accept them. Remember, your behavior may be different from that of other men, but all your particular behaviors fall within the spectrum of normalcy. Okay, okay, I'm not sure what that means either.

Part II: Women—Can't Live With Them . . .

In the first section of Part II, I go under cover and get the straight poop on how women are out to nab, control, and change their men. Direct transcripts reveal the cold and calculating way these women maneuver in for the kill—usually within the first ten minutes of meeting the poor slob!

The second section of Part II breaks all women down into three types, Alpha, Beta, and Gamma, which correspond to the three male types. This will enable you to understand and identify the various personality types. Keep in mind that these techniques range from the subtle to the overt, but the outcome is always the same: *Man*-ipulation.

Part III: Coupling Couples

Introducing the PIG, the Personality Interface Grid, a fancy chart that illustrates each of the possible permutations among our male and female types. Scenarios of the nine potential couplings and interviews with the men in these relationships will divulge the sordid details of how these different types coexist, however uneasily.

The strengths and weaknesses of each coupling are uncovered, so you get a total picture. In these uncensored case histories, you will experience firsthand (sort of) the pathos, bathos, and Porthos of real relationships: starched shirts, overdrawn accounts, empty gas tanks, and other strategies to which women will resort in order to mold their men. *Envy* the sensual and financial heights to which women aspire to make themselves objects of desire. *Cringe* at the depths to which men will succumb to remain normal. *Lust* for the woman who accepts her man the way he is, *and* swallows. *Despair* at the treachery a man will be exposed to when in the clutches of a desperate woman. Find yourself and the woman of your dreams (or nightmares).

Part IV: Can My Type Be Edited?

Probably not. There are plenty of women out there desperate enough to love you as you are. All you have to do is take a look at the statistics: 92 percent of women over thirty have a better chance of being hit by lightning, kidnapped by aliens from another solar system, or becoming president of the United States before the turn of the century than of finding some poor schmuck to take them to the movies on a Tuesday night. And if all you've learned in the end is how to get laid more often and served more home-cooked meals with less grief . . . well, isn't that worth $3.95?

If you really feel the need to change, though, this chapter's for you. Realize, however, that if I had my way, this part would not be included. You're going to have your work cut out for you. You're naive if you think the woman in your life is going to sit back and watch you ruin all the progress she's made in exploiting your life. Hell, do what you gotta do and don't bug me about it if it doesn't work.

Before you proceed to Part I, complete the two questionnaires. They're key to establishing the kind of person you are and the sort of woman to whom you tend to gravitate.

Good luck! And remember, this book's for you.

MALE PROFILE QUESTIONNAIRE

Pick the answer that comes closest to describing your feelings as a male.

1) You would ask a woman to:
   a) pick up your gym clothes, but on second thought realize that was a stupid request and do it yourself;
   b) wash your gym clothes while you make a quiche;
   c) wash, iron, and fold your gym clothes *now*, bitch.

2) You consider husband beating to be:
   a) ridiculous—you dare her;
   b) a frightening but very real phenomenon;
   c) avoidable if lines of communication are properly maintained.

3) The word *poontang*:
   a) makes you consult a dictionary;
   b) makes you blush;
   c) crops up frequently in conversations with your in-laws.

4) If your blind date is not well endowed in the chest department, you:
   a) ditch her at a topless bar;
   b) tactfully suggest silicone implants;
   c) feel pleased she agreed to go out with you anyway.

5) Your wife gets a job offer that would bring her salary well above yours. You:
   a) praise her lavishly and beg for a raise in your allowance;
   b) make it clear it's you or the job;
   c) congratulate her and go sulk in the den.

6) If your lover initiates sexual activity, you:
   a) come in her mouth;
   b) slobber gratefully and wonder what you did right;
   c) act surprised but let her continue.

7) If a recent female acquaintance asks, "What's your sign?" you answer:
   a) "Oh, you probably won't like it";
   b) "Soft Shoulder";
   c) "Pisces, penis rising."

8) If a woman you know calls out of the blue and asks you out to dinner, you:
   a) accept gratefully but feel threatened;
   b) force her to have sex after the meal —she was obviously asking for it;
   c) make sure she doesn't have the wrong number.

9) You're helping your wife do the dishes and you break one by mistake. You:
   a) cringe;
   b) think this is a ridiculous question; you would never be doing the dishes in the first place because you refuse to have anything to do with woman's work;
   c) apologize and clean it up.

10) You find out from your wife that her mother's coming to stay for the week. You:
   a) shout, "No way, bitch!" and blame

her failure to ask permission on female problems;

b) mumble, "Yes, dear," and pick up some extra bandages for yourself in preparation for your mother-in-law's visit;

c) say, "Why that's wonderful, dear," while praying for your mother-in-law's plane to run out of fuel mid-flight.

The scoring of this stupid profile is far more difficult than taking the damn thing. Please bear with me. All you need is a piece of paper, a pencil with a large eraser, a calculator with algebraic function keys, a slide rule, an abacus, and a lot of patience. Or call your accountant. All set? Here goes:

Question 1: a) = 5 pts., b) = 10 pts., c) = 15 pts.

Question 2: a) = 15 pts., b) = 5 pts., c) = 10 pts.

Question 3: a) = 10 pts., b) = 5 pts., c) = 15 pts.

Question 4: a) = 15 pts., b) = 10 pts., c) = 5 pts.

Question 5: a) = 5 pts., b) = 15 pts., c) = 10 pts.

Question 6: a) = 15 pts., b) = 5 pts.,
   c) = 10 pts.
Question 7: a) = 5 pts., b) = 10 pts.,
   c) = 15 pts.
Question 8 a) = 10 pts., b) = 15 pts.,
   c) = 5 pts.
Question 9 a) = 5 pts., b) = 15 pts.,
   c) = 10 pts.
Question 10: a) = 15 pts., b) = 5 pts.,
   c) = 10 pts.

Good job, you're almost done. Now add
up your score and use the following break-
down: if your score is between 125 and 150,
consider yourself an **Able** type; a score of
85–120 points makes you a **Baker** type; 80
points or less, you're a **Charlie** type.

FEMALE PROFILE QUESTIONNAIRE

Pick the answer that comes closest to describing your current relations with women.

1) You come home and tell her you've been laid off. She:
   a) brings up all the household chores you can take over now;
   b) offers to take a second job;
   c) suggests selling one of the kids.

2) You get an invitation to go fishing on the same weekend she's planned a romantic stay for the two of you at a country inn. She:
   a) promises to pack her diaphragm;
   b) makes your life miserable until you decline the invitation;

c) whimpers but concedes you'll probably have more fun fishing.

3) You surprise her with a dress—which
   looks horrible on her. She:
   a) returns it for cash;
   b) wears it all the time to please you;
   c) wears it all the time to annoy you.

4) You want your wife to stay home and
   raise the new baby; she wants to resume
   her career. She:
   a) stays home—she mentioned a job be-
      cause one of her nosy friends put her
      up to it; she's sorry; she'll never do
      it again;
   b) drops the baby off at your office on
      her way to the new job you knew
      nothing about;
   c) works part time and the house is a
      mess.

5) She thinks you're a terrible driver. You
   think she's a menace on the highway.
   You:
   a) drive; she backseat drives;
   b) drive—the Subaru; she drives the
      BMW;

c) drive; she keeps her eyes and mouth
      closed.

6) It's your turn to host the weekly poker
   game with the guys. She:
   a) offers to serve the beer and chips,
      make sandwiches, clean up, etc.;
   b) spends the night elsewhere;
   c) goes along with it—if she can deal.

7) You need that morning bathroom time
   for intellectual pursuits. She needs to
   get ready for work. She:
   a) sets a timer, doesn't care if you get
      hemorrhoids;
   b) does her makeup on the bus;
   c) won't put out until you find an apart-
      ment with two bathrooms.

8) You forget your anniversary. She:
   a) forgets your name but remembers to
      whine about it for weeks;
   b) cries until you spend twice as much
      money on her as you would have in
      the first place;
   c) whimpers and blames herself.

9) You have a big fight over money because you think she's spending too much. She:
   a) agrees and hocks her wedding ring;
   b) agrees, then after you've gone to work, dials the weather in Singapore and leaves the phone off the hook;
   c) disagrees and proves that in fact your monthly expenses exceed hers by 64 percent.

10) You want to make love in the middle of the night. She:
   a) makes *you* try to find her diaphragm;
   b) kicks you in the nuts "by mistake";
   c) sobs until your dick goes limp.

Here we go again with more inane scoring. You've probably figured out from tallying the last questionnaire that neither the slide rule nor the abacus were very much help. Sorry, just a little math humor. I wasn't kidding about the patience part though, huh? Too bad. I'm doing this for you, you know. Believe it or not, I do have better things to do than waste my time teaching you guys how to be normal. I could be watching the SportsChannel on cable, or drinking at the local saloon, or both—hey, what a great idea.

Go ahead and start figuring out your scores. Give me a yell when you're done. Take your time.

Question 1: a) = 5 pts., b) = 15 pts., c) = 10 pts.

Question 2: a) = 10 pts., b) = 5 pts., c) = 15 pts.

Question 3: a) = 10 pts., b) = 15 pts., c) = 5 pts.

Question 4: a) = 15 pts., b) = 5 pts., c) = 10 pts.

Question 5: a) = 5 pts., b) = 10 pts., c) = 15 pts.

Question 6: a) = 15 pts., b) = 10 pts., c) = 5 pts.

Question 7: a) = 10 pts., b) = 15 pts., c) = 5 pts.

Question 8: a) = 5 pts., b) = 10 pts., c) = 15 pts.

Question 9: a) = 15 pts., b) = 5 pts., c) = 10 pts.

Question 10: a) = 10 pts., b) = 5 pts., c) = 15 pts.

The range of scores in this questionnaire is the same as the previous one (thank God). If you score 125–150 points, the type of woman you're attracted to is an **Alpha** type. A score of 85–120 points means you like the **Beta** type. And, finally, 80 points or less describes the **Gamma** type.

Now that that's done, you can move on to the rest of the book safe in the knowledge that I've effectively pigeonholed you and the category of woman you usually latch on to.

PART I

Getting To Know Thyself

If you've completed the questionnaire, you should have an idea of what your type is. "Type?" you ask. "What the hell are you talking about?" Well, after examining all those garbage self-help books, the one valuable lesson I learned was that the authors love to generalize and put the entire female population into manageable groups. So why can't I?

I've devised three oversimplified "types" that incorporate *all* normal males. Instead of the unrelenting type, or the placating type, or even the helpless type, I've chosen to label them Able, Baker, and Charlie; basic and no-nonsense, just like us guys.

But creating three inane types is not enough; you need concrete examples of what it means to be this kind of man. You want to discover that you're not alone. You want to justify your behavior. You want someone to tell you it's okay to be the guy you are. Calm down, that's what this section is for.

After careful research and examination culminating in a tequila binge at La Bamba's Casa de Mexico, I've been able to devise the handy-dandy chart that follows, which shows at a glance each type's strengths and weaknesses.

The following nine, in-depth case histories present three examples of each type. Each case history is broken down into three parts: a brief description of the particular individual in question; a history of his relationship with women; and a summary of his particular situation.

THREE CLASSIC <u>ABLE TYPE</u> PERSONALITIES:

1. *Case History 9384-BH*
Description: At twenty-six years of age, Ed weighs about three hundred pounds and stands only five feet six inches tall. Most of his tonnage is centered in his gut, because

	Strengths	Weaknesses
Able	• Controlling • Forceful • Confident	• Oblivious to nuance • Competitive • Easily frustrated • Quick to anger • Can be manipulated
Baker	• Rational • Smug • Sensitive • Open to change • Relaxed with independent women	• Rational • Smug • Sensitive • Open to change • Relaxed with independent women • Uncertain about role • Guilt-ridden • Can be manipulated
Charlie	• Frank and open • Imaginative • Loyal • Kind • Adaptable	• Gullible • Realistic • Can be manipulated

Ed likes beer, especially while he's on the job as the lube man at the local Gas-and-Crash garage. Known as "Mouth" to all his friends, Ed also enjoys brown-bagging quarts of Genesee cream ale in the park and making loud smacking noises at any woman who passes by while he's feeding arsenic-laced bread crumbs to the pigeons (his only endearing pastime). Ed is a reasonably handsome man despite a cauliflower ear incurred when he was caught flapping his lips at the local state university's All-American linebacker's girlfriend.

History: Ed's been on many dates, but never with the same woman twice. A typical evening starts with Ed picking up his lady on his 1000-cc Harley-Davidson. Unfortunately, his three hundred pounds don't allow much extra room, and his date must squeeze herself between his studded leather jacket and the sissy bar. Once she's settled, Ed usually says something funny, like, "Ooooh, aaahh, do me, baby, till it hurts." Their first stop is the local 7-Eleven, where Ed picks up his-and-hers quarts of Genny for the two-mile ride down to the bowling alley. Ed reserves a lane and rents shoes.

(He has trouble leaning over, so his date must tie the laces for him, which provides him with such comic grist as, "On your knees, bitch," Or "So tell me, do you swallow?") From his vantage point atop a barstool, Ed chugs down massive quantities of beer and smacks his lips loudly as he watches his date's rear end—or dreams of doing so. He has yet to have the pleasure, though, because his dates never stick around that long.

Conclusion: Let's face it. Ed is not what we'd call a ladies' man. He's gross and has absolutely no respect for the "fairer sex." Because he thinks all therapists are faggots, I had a difficult time trying to get Ed to talk to me, until I suggested we move our discussion to the T&A Lounge. He was still leery until I told him I was buying. After about twelve pitchers of Genny, Ed dropped his defenses and shared some of his innermost thoughts. Unfortunately, I got a tiny bit blotto and don't remember a word of the conversation—or how I got home. I woke up in my hotel room the next morning with numerous stud marks across my chest. I can only guess they came from the back of Ed's leather I LOVE HOGS jacket.

Type: Able

2. *Case History: 485-WW*
Description: A single, thirty-year-old stock-broker, Skip had more money than God until the stock market crash in October 1987. Skip has since had to sell his East Hampton summer house and his four-wheel-drive Jeep Cherokee—he refused to part with his 320i BMW, but it's just a matter of time before a collection agency forces the issue—and to cancel his order for six Savile Row seer-sucker and white-linen suits. Now this six-foot-one-inch, 175-pound, blond, blue-eyed wunderkind of the financial world has had to settle for a job as a freelance tax consult-ant to his friends, many of whom also lost their shirts in the crash. He also milks those friends who still have money by peddling junk bonds to them. Skip's hobbies had been squash at New York City's prestigious University Club, sailing his sixty-five-foot Hobie Cat around Long Island Sound, and skeet shooting at Travers Island. Skip's new hob-

bies are watching SportsChannel on cable and sitting on the stoop of his apartment building ogling passing "bimbettes" (Skip's term).

History: After Skip got his M.B.A. from Wharton Business School, he got a job as a junior account executive on a cosmetics account at SSC&B, one of New York City's top ten advertising agencies. Only three months into it he threw the Fax machine at his boss when she yelled at him for not knowing the difference between moisturizer and foundation. Realizing that more and more women were working in the higher echelons of the advertising world, Skip decided to find a job on Wall Street, where women are still referred to as "girls." Skip moved quickly up the financial ladder. Within six months of working at Salomon Brothers, Skip was hauling in major bucks doing insider trading, a little hobby to complement his salary and offset his ever more frequent coke binges. (Skip prided himself on his self-control and only did drugs during those months with the letter *r* in them. Just before the crash he had added the letters *u* and sometimes *y*.)

With money came prestige, and a male chauvinism belying his twenty-two years. Shortly after becoming ensconced at Salomon Brothers, Skip got engaged to a young debutante, but the engagement ended abruptly when he discovered she'd never washed a dish in her life and refused to go down on him during a dull scene of La Bohème. Rumor has it that the real reason was that Skip discovered he was making more money than his fiancée's father. Just prior to the crash, Skip would only date girls from an exclusive "dating service" (high-class hookers with college diplomas and geisha subservience training). Now thirty and penniless, Skip must resort to jerking off and bullying young girls who are "asking for it"—and are too young to have heard of date rape—into cooking him meals and doing his laundry. He pursues these activities with many of his out-of-work stockbroker friends.

Conclusion: Skip gives a new definition to the word *misogyny*. He understands this and is proud of it.

Type: Able

3. _Case History 8425-PPL_

Description: Murray, a television repairman, has been interested in electronics for twenty-five of his forty-one years. He's in incredible shape for his age and regularly exercises his rangy five-foot-nine-inch, 175-pound frame at the local health club. Murray started out in an electronics supply store filling orders for cathode ray tubes, until a friend suggested he learn how to repair TVs. Now Murray has a workshop in his basement and is his own boss. When Murray's not at the club pumping iron, he's out pumping some woman whose TV's on the fritz. Murray's TV Repair 'N' Rental Service is one of the few businesses in the area that still makes house calls.

History: Murray has been married to the same obese brunette for twenty years. They met at the local vocational school, where he majored in refrigeration and minored in advanced car washing, and they were married shortly after graduation. She was training to be a pastry chef but was thrown out when they found fifty pounds of flan mix in her locker. He's very content: she cooks, cleans, and does the windows without complaining. She's also agorophobic (fears open spaces). Consequently this crazy slob never goes out, instead spending her days in front of one of the thirty-odd televisions scattered about the house in various states of disrepair, watching soap operas, and sharing fried pork rinds with her blind parrot, Twinkie, a molting, squawking bird that knows by heart the theme music of "Wheel of Fortune" and is constantly repeating some of the more obnoxious lines from "Search For Tomorrow," "As the World Turns," and "Another World." Murray is free to pursue his out-of-house experiences without worrying about bumping into his wife, and he's away from home a good deal. If Murray isn't out boffing one of his customers or working out at the gym, he can be found trading sexual experiences with his friends at the corner bar, the Baby Doll Club.

Conclusion: Murray thinks smart women are dykes. All the rest fall into two categories: penguins or show dogs. Penguins are ugly, fat, flat-chested women who wait on you hand and foot and give great head, but whom you wouldn't want to be seen with in public. Show dogs, on the other hand, are purely for display. All show dogs have to do is look pretty—they're lousy lays because they don't want their hair, face, or nails mussed. Despite her obvious value, a show dog can quickly fall from status symbol to dyke status if she displays signs of initiative or judgment, or uses big words.

Type: Able

THREE CLASSIC BAKER TYPE PERSONALITIES:

1. *Case History 28-HJU*

Description: A psychotherapist by training, Trope lectures on psychic phenomena at the state college and conducts a seminar on the effects of psychopharmacology and its function as an inhibitor of aggression in cognitive development. Trope is a thirty-six-year-old widower with two adorable kids. He stands five feet seven inches in his stocking feet and weighs 158 pounds. Trope's shoulder-length brown hair, usually tied back in a ponytail, frames a wide, friendly mouth in a perpetual, bemused, I-know-some-thing-you-don't grin; his brown eyes have been described by one of his more poetic students as "two glassy carnelian orbs filled with love."

History: After graduating from Berkeley, Trope lived on a commune for a while, growing macrobiotic vegetables and working in the local food cooperative. There he met Jill, with whom he had two children—a boy and a girl, named Jupiter and Tofu, respectively—out of wedlock. After Trope got busted for selling Quaaludes to an undercover agent at a Tonto's Expanding Headband concert, he decided to "grow up and get a real job." He and Jill got married (barefoot on the beach at Venice) and moved to a small college town in southern California where Trope remains employed by the school.

Unfortunately, a month after they moved, the problems began. According to Trope, Jill couldn't stand the pressures of being a professor's wife in a sleepy college town, even though he did everything possible to help her establish her own career, going out of his way to get her a part-time job as the office manager—she majored in accounting—at the town's only pharmacy. Jealous rumormongers, on the other hand, reported that Jill couldn't deal with Trope's new what-me-worry? and whatever-you-say-dear attitudes to life, the onset of which coincided, as it happens, with the theft of a large quantity of barbiturates from the psychology research lab, a crime unsolved to this day. As the months passed, Jill began drinking heavily, finally committing suicide, leaving a note which said, "I couldn't take that fucking grin of his any longer. A Barcalounger shows more emotion." The campus mourned her death for a week, staging candlelight vigils and poetry readings (the school was hard up for activities). The editor of the school paper wrote an editorial titled, "Woe That We Should Love Too Much and Lose the Love We Lost."

Conclusion: A concerned husband, father, and teacher, Trope may have gotten a bit too carried away by his work. He did spend more and more time in his office at the psych department and could be seen stumbling down the corridor, giggling inappropriately. Committed to his research, he nevertheless had the confidence to encourage Jill's pursuit of a career of her own. (The pharmacist also trusted Jill, giving her the keys to the store, a move which elated Trope.) It wasn't his fault his wife was too narrow-minded to appreciate his gestures of compromise and understanding, not to mention his knowledge of controlled substances.

Type: Baker

2. *Case History 64832-K*
Description: A twenty-four-year-old physical therapist, Mel lives with his girlfriend in a geodesic dome on the outskirts of Boise, Idaho. Mel chose Boise because it's known to attract active young people who love the great outdoors. Mel is an avid bike rider, jogger, and swimmer, and he hopes, once he gets his six-foot frame down to 146 pounds, to compete in his first triathlon. Mel likes to consider himself enlightened and, aside from taking Zen cosmic-power-enlightenment classes at the local college, campaigns regularly for the ERA and other feminist causes.

History: Mel is the son of two nerdy, anemic academics at a highly esteemed city university, where his father teaches quantum physics and his mother heads the math department. Both have short hair, wear thick glasses, and are too cerebral for their own good. A simple conversation about the weather turns into a complicated dissertation about inverse proportions at work in a geometric progression as a passing thunderstorm moves north by northeast into a low-pressure system. After being teased relentlessly by his schoolmates about his fay, androgynous parents, Mel decided that tennis, track, and Frisbee were more fun than English, history, and math, and very possibly more enlightening. Mel's parents occasionally wondered where they'd gone wrong, but only until their attention was captured by a really serious problem, such as the formation of a black hole and its relationship to the superstring theory in particle physics.

You could never accuse Mel of being sexist, because even he had a difficult time telling his parents apart. Mel met his girlfriend at tennis camp when he was sixteen, and they've been close ever since. She works at the local Y teaching swimming to children with Down's syndrome and belongs to the Boise branch of NOW, where Mel volunteers on Tuesday and Thursday nights.

Conclusion: Mel's upbringing was far from normal, but one of the few lessons his parents taught him was that if you get involved in something, get totally involved, though he probably would have been more of his own person if he had pursued a Ph.D. in applied mathematics or physics. So Mel has decided to dedicate his free time to helping women rid themselves of their second-class citizenship. (Mel doesn't realize that someone has to be a second-class citizen and in actuality all he's doing is helping the enemy.) Sometimes Mel's been known to go a bit overboard. On one occasion he lobbied the city to change *manhole cover* to *personhole cover*, and another time, he demanded that the *American Heritage College Dictionary* substitute *Portuguese person-of-war* for *Portuguese man-of-war*.

Type: Baker

3. *Case History 0987-ZSR*

Description: An illustrator of children's books, Jules is forty-three years old and has been happily married to Lucille for twenty of them. Six days of the week, Jules perches his slight, five-foot-one-inch, 105-pound frame atop a five-foot-seven-inch stool so he can reach his drafting table. Jules's studio is located above the garage of their ranch-style home in a quaint rural community on the north shore of Long Island. An avid basketball fan who owns season tickets to all the Knicks home games, Jules also loves to play fast-pitch softball—he leads the league in walks, due to his small strike zone—and he's a competitive limbo dancer.

History: Early on in their relationship, Jules and his wife decided against children; realizing that a vasectomy was far less radical a procedure than tubal ligation, Jules volunteered. Their decision was predicated on the fact that Jules didn't want to foist upon another generation the same ridicule he had endured. A "late bloomer" until his senior year in college, Jules stood only four feet six inches tall. Another slightly more selfish reason, which came out during therapy, has to do with Lucille's gene pool: she's five-eleven, and Jules refused to contemplate eventually wearing his offspring's hand-me-downs.

Conclusion: Jules walks a fine line between the Able and Baker personalities. His height hang-up is justifiable for a male, and he addresses the subject with candor. Very competitive, he's into sports and uses his handicap to advantage. But let's face it—he's a shrimp. (Just don't call him that to his face, because he'd probably punch out your kneecaps.) On the other hand, Jules's choice of vocation speaks of a gentler, kinder side to the man. Children are not as easily fooled as grown-ups, and Jules's drawings are a favorite among the younger set. The deciding factor is Jules's decision to have a vasectomy: no Able type would ever consider having his dick notched to shoot blanks.

Type: Baker

THREE CLASSIC CHARLIE TYPE PERSONALITIES:

1. *Case History 143-RR*
Description: Justin is a thirty-two-year-old veterinarian who lives at home with his mother. When he's not rushing to her bedside like one of Pavlov's dogs every time she rings her bell, he's busy vacuuming, doing the dishes, and generally straightening up the house. For fun, Justin compares different kinds of silverware polish and rearranges the spice rack. Not unattractive, Justin has naturally curly brown hair, large blue eyes, and stands a lanky six feet four inches tall. Unfortunately, he weighs only 125 pounds, and on more than one occasion has been mistaken for a praying mantis, albeit a handsome one.

History: Due to his mother's protracted illness of undetermined origin, Justin hasn't had much time for dating. In fact, by some strange coincidence, every time Justin has made a date with some woman from work —such as the time he asked out Doris, a large-mammal anesthesiologist—his mother experiences a sudden relapse and Justin has to cancel. The one time Justin actually did go out (his mother had been complaining of amnesia for a day and a half and kept mistaking him for her long-lost pet Chihuahua, Fudgenut), it was an utter disaster. According to Justin, everything was going smoothly until she answered the door and stuck out her hand to shake his. Justin instinctively slapped a blood pressure cuff on her arm and, due to overexcitement, overinflated it, cutting off so much blood that she passed out. Justin tried to revive his date with mouth-to-mouth resuscitation, but when she regained consciousness all she could do was scream rape. Not knowing how to react, Justin bayed at the moon for a moment or two and fled.

Conclusion: Justin is a victim of his environment—or more specifically, of his mother's hypochondria. Of course, he has angry "feelings" toward his mom, but instead of telling her where to go, Justin would rather not deal with the problem. Justin would probably be happier if he could give up all human social interaction and just concentrate on his little buddies from the animal kingdom. Under hypnosis, Justin admitted that he masturbates to *Pet House* magazine and that his ultimate fantasy is setting up house with ewe-know-who.

Type: Charlie (by default)

2. *Case History 1492-RSV*

Description: At forty, Milton is a short, pudgy, hairy CPA who collects pumpkin-seed art. The highlight of his weekend is watching "Pee-Wee's Playhouse" (he's the only person over five years old who actually screams whenever the secret word comes up). Milton has never said no to his wife and frequently sports a memento of her affection in the form of a limp or a black eye.

History: Surprisingly enough, Milton's on his third wife; his first one ran off with the defensive line of the Tampa Bay Buccaneers and his second is now living in a lesbian relationship with her karate instructor. Milton met his current wife at the 1984 Summer Olympics, where she won a bronze medal lifting weights for her mother country, Rumania, defecting to the U.S. immediately afterward. Their first encounter took place in the basement of the Olympic Village, where Milton, representing the accounting firm of Janowitz, Epstein, & Jones, was auditing the books for possible discrepancies by one of the nephews of a friend of the assistant swimming coach.

Conclusion: Milton Brodski's—oops; forget you saw that last name—favorite sexual activity is fantasizing about being a sex slave for a tribe of busty Amazons. If he's having sex, he's usually on the bottom—his preference. And there's always a woman in his life, because if there weren't, who'd pick on him? Milton is a classic example of a pussy-whipped male.

Type: Charlie

3. _Case History 00667-CFV_
Description: Sydney is a twenty-five-year-old, 101-pound, five-foot-five-inch concert pianist for a large philharmonic orchestra in a city in the Midwest. He's single and lives in a spacious one-bedroom condo overlooking Lake Michigan with his cocker spaniel, Chopin. Chopin and Sydney are insepara-

ble, and Sydney has been known to ask the dog for advice on financial matters and musical preferences. For enjoyment, Sydney and Chopin take turns chasing sticks in the park outside their building and playing duets on the piano. (Chopin has learned "Chopsticks" and is working on "Frère Jacques.")

History: Sydney's been playing piano ever since his parents found him sitting in the corner of the living room with his arms outstretched, fingers twitching in midair. After placing a borrowed typewriter in front of the three-year-old with disastrous results, they picked up a toy piano from the Salvation Army, and Sydney proceeded to play J. S. Bach's Chromatic Fantasia and Fugue in D Minor. A prodigy was born. From that day on, Sydney played his piano from dawn to dusk. His parents, unaccustomed to this type of behavior and hoping they could make some money out of it, wanted to sell him to the local circus, but cooler heads prevailed and he was awarded a scholarship at the Chicago Conservatory of Music. After coming in second in Russia's prestigious International P. I. Tchaikovsky Competition, he was asked to join the Chicago Philharmonic. Sydney's one date was with a policewoman from the Chicago PD Canine Squad, whom he met at O'Hare International after completing a European tour. She was at customs checking luggage for controlled substances when Chopin and Rex, a large German shepherd, struck up a conversation. One thing led to another, and the two owners made a date to go out to a White Sox game, her idea. The date ended in tragedy when Rex tried to mount Chopin during the seventh-inning stretch. Rex and Chopin never saw each other again.

Conclusion: Sydney's behavior was very tough on his parents, who couldn't understand how this working-class boy could possibly enjoy spending his free time in front of that stupid toy piano day after day playing "that classical stuff." They've got a point. Anyone who voluntarily chooses to practice scales when he could be outside playing stickball or stealing hubcaps won't find the time to pursue women. The guy's either a homo, a nerd, or a wimp.

Type: Charlie

PART II

Women—Can't Live With Them . . .

Before we explore the basic pairings, let's go back to the beginning: the first time a woman lays eyes on her man. Here are six women who've been kind enough to share their experiences about a particular man they were attracted to and why. Less interesting here than the discussion of type, though, is the question of change. Of course, these ladies aren't about to admit the real reasons behind their attachments, nor how, ultimately, every one of these attractions was predicated on changing the male into a gratifying flunky. Before most of us know what's hit us, the woman is busy jockeying for position. Usually within ten minutes of the first encounter, she has us pegged and headed for slaughter.

Compromise is not part of the female lexicon. Oh, they have us believing that they want to meet us halfway regarding our habits and life-styles, but it's not the case. Unfortunately, we seldom realize it until it's too late—if we realize it at all. While all we're doing is hoping we might get lucky on that first date, she's already picking out the damn wallpaper for the kid's room. Or figuring how to get us to work two jobs so she can spend more of our money. Or screwing us until she's squeezed us dry and then tossing us away like so much garbage! OR CUTTING OUT OUR SOULS WITH A BLUNT BUTTER KNIFE AND STOMPING ALL OVER THEM WITH HER STORM–TROOPER BOOTS AS SHE SMILES SWEETLY AND TELLS US HOW BIG OUR MUSCLES ARE! YEAH, SALLY, I'M TALKING TO YOU, YOU BITch . . . Oh, ahh . . . sorry . . . got a bit carried away. Anyway, this section provides crucial insight into detaching and identifying those hidden agendas.

Note: In order to win the confidence of these women, I had to go undercover. Raiding a friend's closet, I found a wonderful muted paisley skirt that fit like a glove. Luckily, I had an understated but elegant string of pearls and matching earrings. The shoes were a bit problematic because I haven't had much practice wearing heels, but after a harrowing hour at the Tall Gal's Shoe Tree, I found a very comfortable pair of espadrilles. To make my disguise complete, I changed my name to Cassiopeia and told the interviewees I was working on a book for women called *Man as Utility Tool*.

FATAL ATTRACTIONS/ HIDDEN AGENDAS

Fatal Attraction #1
Subject: Bunny
Age: 40
Occupation: Waitress

"Cassiopeia, that's a strange name. Are you an actress or something? You're pretty big-boned; do you eat a lot of red meat? Never mind.

"Let's see. I met Bruno while I was working the night shift at Bobby Lee Bob's Greasy

Spoon and Eats Emporium. The minute he walked in I knew he was the man for me. He sidled up to the counter, settled his cute, tight butt down on the stool and picked up the menu. Whooee! That man's chest could stop a train, and his pecs would put Stallone's to shame. So what if he had a bit of a beer belly? I'm no beauty queen myself, you know. His puppy-dog eyes and wavy hair were brown. Even the shit-eating grin turned me on. Even though he refused to look me in the face, I could tell he noticed me, but I wasn't going to push it. When I asked him what he wanted, he mumbled something about a cup of coffee and a prune Danish. I said fine and dandy and brought him a cup of my special herbal tea and a bowl of bran flakes. (You can never be too regular.) Well, you should have seen the look on that man's face when I put his food down in front of him. He scratched his head, looked real perplexed, like, and asked the bran flakes what they were doing there. I explained to him the benefits of being regular and how there wasn't an ounce of nutrition in a piece of Danish and how cholesterol can gum up your works. I also told him about the evils of coffee and how it's done in more folks than Hiroshima.

"While he was eating, we got to talking. Turned out he hauled eggs down from Massachusetts. Well, I told him that he was transporting hundreds of thousands of potential time bombs. Eggs are killers, everybody knows that. I also hinted that it might be a good idea if he stopped driving a truck and picked up a job that offers a bit more security. You know—like something in life insurance. You're not going to live forever.

"Oh, yeah, back to the first time. Well, I'll be damned if he didn't just eat that bowl of bran right up. Drank up the tea, too—made a face, though. After that he started coming into the diner regular, and he let me order his food for him. Well, that was the first time I met Bruno, and I'll never forget it. I wish I could, though. After four years of bliss, he ran away with my best friend, Madge. She worked over at the Donut Hole. Talk about your killers. Why, they dunk those things in coconut oil—that's a saturated fat, and it can really clog your pipes. . . .

"Oh, you got enough information? Good. If I can be of any further help for your book, you let me know. Hey, did I ask you if you ate a lot of red meat? I did? Well, you should take care of yourself. Lay off the calcium. Your bones are big enough."

The Hidden Agenda: Bunny's hidden agenda is rather obvious, as were her snide comments. My bones're just right, thank you very much.

See how she operates? She was working on changing me just like she was working on poor Bruno from the minute he walked into the diner. (All right, I was in disguise, but I could feel she sensed something.)

Let's face it, at that point in her life, anybody with two legs would have suited Bunny just fine. Unfortunately, all poor Bruno wanted to do was have a cup of coffee and a Danish. Instead, he was the sole contestant on *Bunny's Dating Game*. Bruno had the last laugh. He didn't dump her until he'd lost his beer belly, his cholesterol count was the lowest it's ever been, and his blood pressure was a safe 120 over 80.

Subject: Babs
Age: 32
Occupation: Independently wealthy

"Hmmm . . . I must admit, Cassiopeia, I've never seen a size eighteen dress worn with such flair. Must have cost a fortune—all the fabric, you know. You *must* tell me who designed it. Omar the Tentmaker? Sorry, dear, just a little joke. I *do* hope I didn't embarrass you. Do you know that when you blush your facial hair stands out? Estée Lauder has a wonderful foundation that'll cover *anything* up. Just trying to help. All right, all right, don't get so prickly. Here's my fascinating experience.

"You might find it difficult to believe, but money bores me. If you *must* know, the only reason I'll deign to discuss such a vulgar subject is because it's the only topic my working friends seem *comfortable* with. Luckily for me I can stomach small doses. Speaking of doses, I'll just pop a Valium.

"You don't want to talk about money?

"My initial feelings about one of the *men* in my life? Well, I don't know if that's any of your business. Are you from *People* magazine? Hmmm . . . A book for *women*, you say? I guess I can help you, but you *must* promise not to print my name—unless I say something *terribly* witty.

"Well, let me see . . . ah, yes; I could tell you about darling Pablo. I met him on the beach at Cannes a few years ago. I was enjoying the cool breezes that swept past and watching an exquisite sunset over the yacht basin when he walked by my chaise longue, spitting and swearing at no one in particular. I *must* admit that I was quite amused and asked if I could buy him a drink. *Well,* he was dressed à la Don Johnson, in a stained white linen suit over a smelly black T-shirt that he must have been wearing since morning! He hadn't shaved for at least a week, but he *was* cute. French and dissolute—you know, the Jean-Paul Belmondo type. Though I think he purchased his clothes off the rack—*un peu gauche, n'est-ce pas?*

"At the bar, he drank his vodka and I sipped my dry vermouth with a twist. It was then I discovered Pablo was an artist. I think his medium was oils or acrylics or polyester, something like that. Whatever. *Well,* I gradually became quite attracted to him; something about that raw, masculine odor he exuded, like a caged panther in season. One thing led to another, and he ended up coming back to the States with me. I introduced him to *all* of my friends, and we were the envy of my group. Tragically, his drinking got the best of him, and he died after consuming a quart of bourbon in half an hour. Could have been sticky, but fortunately the chief of police is a dear, dear friend.

"Oh, here, would you like to see a picture of my new racehorse? He's Arabian, and his name is Scimitar, or Samovar, something exotic like that. The trainer tells me he's *très* fast.

"Don't mention it. I'm glad I was able to share my deepest inner feelings with you. My shrink will be *so* pleased.

"I *do* apologize for the comments about your dress, but I thought it would be better to say something than to watch you walk around making an *utter* fool of yourself. My shrink wants me to express my feelings more; I'm not paying him one hundred twenty bucks an hour for my health, you know. I'm okay, you're ugly. Ha, ha—hey, what *are* you doing? Take your hairy hands from around my throat. I can't brea—"

Hidden Agenda: Don't worry, I didn't hurt the stuck-up bitch. But don't think I didn't want to. What does she know about fashion, anyway? Or about people, for that matter? Sure, she'll probably let somebody fuck her, but neither party will have much fun. Babs is desperate to own things, and in this case it was Pablo she wanted.

A little research revealed that Babs's hidden agenda had to do with her best friend Mindy, who had picked out a young German poet earlier that summer and was trotting him around the New York literary circuit. Babs, that overbred snob, couldn't wait to see the look on Mindy's face when she hit town with an authentically crazy French— I found out later the guy was born in Trenton, New Jersey—artsy-fartsy misanthrope.

Pablo couldn't deal with the jet set lifestyle, and, true to form, Babs got bored after the novelty wore off. Her only regret is that he totaled the Porsche 911 during his drunken spree. Luckily the autopsy revealed he was dead before the car went out of control, and her lawyers think they can get the insurance company to replace the car ("I hated the color, anyway"). What a spoiled bitch! Damn,

I shouldn't have taken my hairy hands off of her neck so soon.

Fatal Attraction #3
Subject: Suzie
Age: 25
Occupation: Aerobics teacher

"Gee whiz, Cassiopeia, you should get out and exercise more. Don't take this the wrong way, but, like, you look like you're seven months pregnant. Cheer up, though; you're the first woman I ever met who doesn't have hips. Unfortunately, those saddlebags are tough to get rid of. Have you ever taken steroids? I don't have to tell you how bad they are for you, do I? Naughty, naughty, Cassiopeia. That could be the reason why you've got so much facial hair. Like, are you Italian? Maybe you should think about getting your face waxed or something.

"I'm sorry, I didn't mean to hurt your feelings, but you really should take care of your body. It's the only one you have.

"For sure, we can talk about Bobby now. Bobby was a real dream. He was tall and handsome, and could he dance. Geez, I met Bobby at a disco in Cleveland. It wasn't really a disco—that was in the seventies. Now they call it a dance club. Isn't that funny? Same thing, different name. Oh, yeah, Bobby. I'll never forget. He asked me to dance and, boy, did we have fun, fun, fun!

"He had all the right moves—you know, another John Travolta. The only problem was that he dressed that way, too. You know what I mean? White pants, white jacket, black imitation satin shirt, usually open to the navel, with a collar so pointy it could draw blood, and white vinyl loafers. Yecch! Let's face it, the man was a walking cliché. He even wore like twelve heavy gold chains. Golly, many nights, after hours of nonstop dancing, the poor guy's upper body was one big bruise. He was losing a lot of chest hair, too.

"The first time I saw Bobby, the clothes grossed me out, but there was something about him that kept me kind of interested —and don't forget, he was a great dancer. After a while on the dance floor, I nearly forgot about his clothes and had a really neat time. We exchanged phone numbers, but I didn't expect him to call. Surprise, surprise, he called me the very next day, and we agreed to meet that evening at the club. I can't tell you how excited I was. During lunch break I went out to get a granola bar at Noel's Health Food Cooperative, and on my way, I passed by a Benetton store and saw the greatest sweatshirt in the window, a white and gold cotton pullover that said Camp Beverly Hills on the front. Well, without a second thought, I went inside and bought it for Bobby.

"Was he surprised! I wasn't sure if he was going to like it, so I burst into tears when he opened the package. I guess I was nervous. He made a bit of a face, but he put it on anyway, and boy, he looked great! I stopped crying and we danced the night away.

"We had a wonderful time and made a date to meet at the new shopping center that just opened up in Brecksville—that's a suburb south of Cleveland. I told him I'd be waiting in front of the Reebok window display at Sneakers 'N' Things. Well, he was right on time, and four hours, two hundred fifty dollars, and three tearful scenes—me, not him, silly—later, Bobby was a new man. He looked just like Kool Moe Dee—he's my favorite rap singer.

"Like, I guess that's all. By the way, Cassiopeia, is this book of yours like, a, you know, a self-help book for us girls? And what do you mean by "man as utility tool"? Is it going to be like a workout book? If it is, I'd go on a diet or something before you go on any of the talk shows. I'm sorry to say it, but you're not the world's best advertisement for a book about being in shape. And stay away from steroids."

The Hidden Agenda: If you don't mind, Susie, I happen to be right in the range for big-boned people my height. Anyway, I'm not here to talk about my problems.

So who are we kidding? Susie found a guy whose idea of fashion differs drastically from her own. But, instead of taking the guy for what he is, she felt compelled to change him—literally.

After further conversations with Susie, I found out that the order of events after their first meeting was actually a little different.

Turns out she not only knew he was going to call her, she had purchased the Benetton shirt *prior* to his call. Confident little minx, wouldn't you say? Even I admit the tears were a stroke of genius. What better way to get a man to do your bidding than to open the floodgates (not that a man could use the same trick without appearing weak, unmasculine, and/or faggy)? Susie's ingenuity didn't end with the tears, though. Notice how she chose the Reebok window display for their first nondancing rendezvous? Talk about your hidden agendas!

In less than two months' time, Bobby's wardrobe experienced a dramatic reversal: his shirts were now light-colored and cotton, and his suits either blue, black, or charcoal gray. This only goes to show that the man may wear the pants in the family, but the woman probably picked them out.

By the way, they were married three months after this interview took place. Bobby's mother wasn't allowed to attend the wedding unless she took Susie with her to find something "suitable" to wear at Loehmann's; Bobby's father wore a rented black tux, luckily for him.

Fatal Attraction #4:
Subject: Bridget
Age: 20
Occupation: Student

"Cassiopeia, groovy name. What's your sign? Do you have a cold or something, Cassiopeia? Your voice is real low. You sound like my father. Pop says that some men find a real low voice in a woman sexy. Well, is it? Do a lot of guys hit on you? Chill out, don't take it so personal. I just asked a simple question.

"I know what's really bothering you: all that gross hair on your knuckles, right? Listen, my friend Sasha says that you can buy these depilatories. You rub 'em all over the places where the hair's the worst and it should make it disappear. You might want to shave the big patches of hair first, with a Bic razor or something. You know, like your knuckles. The creams don't work all that well. Yeeecch. Sorry.

"Okay, okay, I'll tell you about Charles. Cool your jets. Boy, are you oversensitive.

"Charles was quite the BMOC: tall, handsome, and the first-string quarterback. We met at a homecoming game, which was kind of strange, because I hated jocks and usually hung around with the heads. While the jocks, frat boys, and rah-rah sorority girls were busy chanting at the pep rally like a bunch of demented cannibals, we were tripping our brains out and watching the pretty colors of the bonfire from the roof of the campus center.

"I still don't know how we ended up at the game. All I remember is that I was still real high from the second hit of purple microdot. I have no idea how they play football, but it didn't matter. From up in the bleachers it looked like a group of black ants battling a group of red ants for a crumb of pumpernickel bread. Pretty weird, huh?

"Just before the game ended, my friends decided to go into the nearby woods and play in the cemetery, but since I was still getting off on the warrior ants, I stayed behind. I remember looking over at the scoreboard and grooving on the hands of the game clock as they went round and round. Suddenly someone was tapping me on the shoulder. It was Charles. He asked me if I was all right, because the game had been over for an hour. That probably explains why the hands of the clock had stopped dancing.

"He sat down next to me. I had already peaked, but the acid had a lot of speed in it, so I was really talkative. He laughed when I asked him who won, and that got me laughing, too—I felt like a real jerk. He explained some of the rudimentaries of football and told me how he had been given a football scholarship and how he hoped to go professional. I freaked, because while I was watching the insects, I remembered seeing the red ant—the one that got the bread crumb from the rear end of the ant in front of him—being jumped on and squashed by the black ants from the other team. It didn't look fun. You want to get beaten up for a living? I asked. Even though I was as high as a kite, I knew I'd touched a raw nerve, so I let the topic drop. I was going to let him drop, too, but he had an okay sense of humor and a real nice bod. He had been thinking along the same lines, because out of the blue he asked me if I wanted to go to a movie with him. Sure, I said, why not? We had a good time. I made sure not to bring up the topic of football as a profession, and instead I introduced him to the world of controlled substances. He saw the light in no time. Unfortunately, we broke up before graduation, when he got busted buying cocaine and had to do a year's time. I tried to wait, but Daddy said if I stopped seeing him, he'd buy me that mint-condition 1968 Corvette Stingray I had my eye on.

"Cassy, are you into astrology? Maybe the stars can lead you along a less hairy path to enlightenment. Face the facts—hairy knuckles don't make it."

The Hidden Agenda: Astrology?! "Groovy"?! "Cassy"?! Where does this throwback to the Seventies get off criticizing how *I* look? She was wearing so much fringe and beads, she looked like something out of Cher's song "Half-breed" ("Gypsies, tramps, and thieves . . ."). I'd rather be hairy than a space cadet. I think she used a depilatory on her brain. Enough about that.

It's pretty obvious what Bridget thought about football, which is one big strike against her to start with. Even on a hallucinogen like LSD, this woman wanted to work over Charlie's future, although she had the presence of mind to realize a blitz on his life's dream might not be the best approach. Instead she opted for the more subtle end-around run: she introduced him to drugs and let him punt his career. If he hadn't been nabbed by the cops, Bridget would have probably married the guy, and you can bet he wouldn't have been playing football for a living. Now that he's serving time, Bridget's last comment was, "Charlie who?" Thank God for Daddy.

Like most women, Bridget knows how to cut her losses. So instead of wasting time moping over Charlie's loss to the California State penal system, Bridget bravely forged ahead. Now father and daughter are both happy. She's found a wonderful new boyfriend whom her daddy adores—he's a lawyer with a lot of money—and she's got someone who will keep her nose stuffed with cocaine while they cruise down the San Fernando Valley at 120 miles per hour in the Stingray.

Note: Fathers of daughters are notorious for realigning their priorities. When it comes down to choosing between one's fellow man

and Daddy's little princess, male bonding
goes out the window.

Fatal Attraction #5
Subject: Ruth
Age: 35
Occupation: Housewife

"It is Cassiopeia, isn't it? Well . . . may I
ask you a question? Is that your real hair?
I, ah, don't mean to pry or anything, but
that wig could use some work. Oh, what
am I saying? But it is a wig, isn't it? I thought
so. You see, I could tell by the coloring; it's
different from the color of your sideburns
—oh, no! Did I say sideburns? I meant the
hair on the side of your head. Oh, I __am__
sorry. Here let me give you the name of a
friend who makes wigs from human hair.
It looks so much more lifelike than those
finely woven plastic strands.

"You're quite right—we're not here to talk
about your hair, we're here to talk about my
Lester. Ah . . . Lester, Lester, Lester. He's
the first and last man I've ever loved, the

father of my beautiful children, and the breadwinner.

"We've been married, let me see, almost fifteen years now. Hard to believe, isn't it? They've been happy years for me. A lot of women can't understand why I like being a housewife, but I don't care what they think. I never wanted some stupid old career. If being a mother and housewife was good enough for my mom, then it's good enough for me. Oh yes, you want to know where I first met Lester. Well . . . ah . . . let me see if I can remember. I think it was in the local A&P. At the . . . ah . . . the frozen foods section, if I'm not mistaken. Yes, that's definitely right, right between the Green Giant Oriental vegetable medley and the Swanson turkey pot pies. I remember, because Lester was a bachelor then, and I knew single men live on TV dinners, especially Swanson's frozen Hungry-Man dinners. The chicken dinner is the most popular.

"As soon as I saw him round the aisle past the Comet and other home cleaning products, I knew he was the man for me. Oh, I could tell he was single as soon as I saw him. You see, he was carrying one of those plastic baskets instead of pushing a shopping cart, a sure sign of shopping for one. He also had a perplexed look on his face, like, ah, someone who doesn't go to supermarkets very often.

"I'll never forget that dirty ring around his collar, or how rumpled his pants were. And if I'm not mistaken, I seem to remember that he had two different-colored socks on. Isn't that just adorable? What really won me over was his kind face and the gentle way he carried himself. I saw him wave at a child in a shopping cart that was going in the opposite direction. Like a flash it hit me: perfect breeding stock.

"Let's see. . . . My suspicions about his marital status were confirmed when he opened the door to the freezer and grabbed, what was it? . . . at least six Hungry-Man dinners, two beef and four chicken. I snuck a peek at his basket and noticed a head of iceberg lettuce, a small jar of mayonnaise, a six-pack of Stroh's beer, a package of Oreos, three bags of Doritos, and a can of Planters beer nuts.

"I guess I was busy peeking, because all of a sudden the front wheel of my cart rolled over his left foot. You can imagine my embarrassment. Of course he said he was okay and that I should think nothing of it, you know. You won't believe what happened next, though. In all the excitement of apologizing, a five-pound can of crushed tomatoes mysteriously fell out of my cart and guess where it landed. Right on his other toe! I was mortified!

"Everything worked out for the best, you know. After the hospital set his toe—they have to put on a cast if it's your big toe (his driving foot, if you can believe it)—I took him to my apartment for a nice dinner. I guess you could say the rest was history.

"Well, ah, I hope I was of some assistance. And if I can help you get a new wig, you just let me know. Oh, by the way, make sure you stay away from open flames, because those synthetic fibers can go up like there's no tomorrow."

The Hidden Agenda: Wig, schmig! I do the best I can, and what happens? No wonder women have self-esteem problems. I'd like to see Ruth try to dress up like a man. On second thought, I'd rather not.

I certainly learned one thing from Ruth, and that's not to mess around. Here's a woman with determination. Lester was the fly, Ruth the spider, and the web was the A&P. Ruth not only knew the store, but she was aware of the buying habits of single men. How did she know that the chicken TV dinners sold better than the other TV dinners? Let's face it, she would have made an awesome marketing analyst. All she had to do was position herself and let the unsuspecting men come to her.

Don't be fooled by her "ahs" and "hmms." She knew exactly how the story went—she wrote the script! You've probably realized that the wayward shopping cart and convenient five-pound can of crushed tomatoes were no accident, but did you know that the shopping cart with the kid had also been staged? Scary, isn't it?

Fatal Attraction #6
Subject: Helen
Age: 84
Occupation: Retired

"Isn't Cassiopeia a woman's name? Well, then, why are you going by a woman's name? And why are you all dressed up in that silly costume? You look like one of them monkeys in the circus that they put clothes on so they look human. Are you one of them transvestites or something? Never met a real transvestite before. What? You're under cover? I don't see any cover, but maybe that's a good idea. The fewer people who see you the better.

"Don't yell at me, young man. I'll tell my story when I'm good and ready. [pause]

"I don't remember too good these days. Let me see. I guess the last relationship I remember was with Bernie. I met him here in the home some time after Sidney died. My rotten, good-for-nothing kids put me here. They said I was forgetting to do things like . . . like . . . Oh, who cares. It's funny, some things I can remember like they happened yesterday, while others, like the day of the week, I couldn't answer if my next bingo jackpot depended on it. Now, what was that question again? Bingo? Oh, yes, Bernie. I remember meeting Bernie here at the home, about three months ago—right after those rotten children of mine had me locked up in here. That Bernie was a real card. I remember the first time I called him a card, he said he should be dealt with. I think I laughed.

"It was in the dayroom here. I recollect it was midmorning and time for our regular gin rummy game. Bernie had been admitted the week before and was trying to get the lay of the land. Nurse Numbnuts—that's my pet name for her—rolled Bernie right up to our table and put on the wheel lock. After Numbnuts introduced us all around, I could see Bernie was taking a shine to that whore Gloria and her tasteless friends, Myron and Edgar. I had decided—I think—that Bernie was going to have nothing to do with the likes of those.

"Just before rest period, Nurse Thunderthighs—yes, another of my pet names—gave out the midday medication. Our pills would be sitting in neat little rows in small paper cups with our names handwritten on tiny cards in front of the cups, just inside the door to the dayroom. I took the round blue pill out of Gloria's cup, buried it in a nearby flowerpot that supported this ugly, spindly, dying, spider plant, sat back, and watched. Thirty minutes later poor old Gloria was bouncing off the walls. Funniest thing I'd ever seen. She was singing "My Darling Clementine" one minute and blubbering about the death of her dog, Precious, the next. I tell you, I got a stiff neck just watching her. And the spider plant put out three shoots the next day.

"It worked perfectly. Bernie was afraid to go anywhere near the poor crazy woman, and I made sure I made myself available to comfort him and explain her condition. Now, don't you quote me, young man, but I think that's how it all happened.

"Next time, young man, don't come sneaking in here dressed like a lady—especially if you can't pull it off."

The Hidden Agenda: No fear, lady. If our paths never cross again, I'll be happy.

Well, as you could probably tell, Helen has a mind like a steel trap. Notice how she remembered all the events leading up to Gloria's freak-out, from the color of the pill to the description of the plant. Her "memory problem" is her way of getting sympathy and attention. It was going to be her approach to Bernie, until Gloria got in the way.

I found out later that her kids had put her into a home because she was a real pain in the ass. I also found out that Sidney died under mysterious circumstances. Of course, no one could pin anything on her.

Finally, did you realize how blatant she was? Unlike some of the other, younger women I spoke to, Helen knew exactly what she was doing. She wanted Bernie, and nobody was going to keep her from getting him—not even Bernie. He'd find out soon enough.

DESCRIPTIONS OF FEMALE TYPES

Now that you have an idea how manipulative *all* women are, let's take a closer look at the different female types.

Alpha Type

The Alpha personality type is the easiest to identify and to understand, but so what; she still drives men crazy. Women in this category are tough and can usually go the distance. They won't put up with any shit and have no qualms about letting you know when you've screwed up.

1. *Interview 421-XT*

Anita is a thirty-three-year-old meat packer and the ex-wife of one of my patients. Below is a typical example of her direct approach.

"What a bastard! Can you believe he really thought I wouldn't find out what he was doing with that bimbo of a secretary? Sure, he says nothing happened. Then how come I found them alone in his office? It looked innocent enough. He was sitting behind his desk and the little tramp was in a chair across from him taking dictation. Bullshit! More like dick-tation.

"Huh? No, I didn't catch him in the act, you fool. My husband's dumb, but not that dumb."

Don't waste your subtlety on me. A tough little cookie, wouldn't you say? As you can see, Anita is not one to mince words, and her behavior is a classic example of the Alpha type, who loves to come out fighting. For her, a good defense is a real good offense, and her words are more effective than any punch in the mouth or slap upside the head. An Alpha type is efficient. She knows that getting physical can drain your energy quicker than a sharp tongue. That's the only reason she doesn't come out punching: her tactic is staying power.

2. *Interview 296-LS*

Forty-four-year-old Hildi gives me a massage once a week. She was kind enough to agree to tell me a little about herself during one of our sessions.

"I like to give the massage. It feels-a good to—how you say—push and prod the flabby, fleshy parts of the flaccid and disgusting overweight men.

"My first husband, Gunther, had a good body, until he started eating all that cherry strudel. He got very big and round, and I tell him to stop being pig or I leave him. I make him go on diet, but he sneak pieces of strudel every time I don't look.

"When he was sleeping, I hold him down and a friend wire his mouth shut. No more strudel. No more Gunther, either. He had terrible strudel withdrawals, jumped into the Yser, and sank like a stone.

"His lack of self-discipline make me so mad, I want to squeeze his neck so tight. . . . Oh, sorry Mr. Evans. Don't worry, will disappear in a week or so. Wear turtlenecks."

What we won't do in the name of research. I was one big bruise after that rub-down. As you could see, Hildi is a good example of a strong-willed individual with physical strength to match. Never again!

Beta Type

A Beta type is the worst: she's the most difficult to identify and the hardest to catch in the act. A Beta personality type is very manipulative, in fact often schizophrenic, and usually smarter than her mate. One minute she wants to be an independent woman of the Nineties, competing with her male counterparts for that next lunge up the corporate ladder; the next, she feels guilty for not being attached to a male provider so she can stay home and raise a family.

Before you start feeling sorry for her, realize that the Beta type is smart enough to compensate. She has come to the unique conclusion that the best way to have both a career and a family is to marry someone dumber than she is. This way she can still keep her hand in the business world and her knees in his back.

1. *Interview 793-PO*

Thirty-nine-year-old Deborah is a bonds trader for a major brokerage house and someone I met one night at a singles bar for pathetnoids. She was in a particularly fragile state, and I was able to get some juicy insights into her personality type. Beta, natch.

"I like my life just as it is. [*sob*] I wouldn't trade places with anyone. Would you like to see pictures of my younger sister's children? They're beautiful. My last boyfriend? Well, he was a really nice guy. Unfortunately he was a teacher and made 12.75 percent of my *net* prebonus salary. We tried not to let that get in the way, but, come on, how much domestic champagne can you drink? It gives me such a headache. And it was either a bottle of Dom or his rent.

"What would I do differently next time?

I'd find someone who shared my priorities but was in less of a strategic bargaining position. Then I'd leverage a deal that would give me financial security and the opportunity to procreate. Of course, I'd cover my position with a golden parachute clause and a poison-pill provision in the event some aggressive female tried a hostile takeover.''

Of course, the Beta type has not come to grips with the fact that she can't have a family unless she punts her career aside and spends three years scraping dried, cement-hard Pablum off her charcoal gray Ann Taylor three-piece suits (which she'll need to try on occasionally to stave off clinical depression). Or she can always entrust her little darling to the care of someone who grew up barefoot on a tropical island, and learn the virtues of ''quality time'' as she tries to snatch a free minute to take a meeting with her own kid. But she'll give it her best shot; she's so driven it's disgusting.

2. *Interview 989-MN*
At thirty years old, Connie is a housewife

and mother of two. Her husband was one of my patients, until Connie calmly walked into my office and quietly suggested I stop treating him. I agreed immediately without asking why—thank God. With this Beta type, you have to really read between the lines.

"Bob's a good provider, I just wish he'd realize how important politics is. He's an account supervisor at a large advertising agency, but he could easily handle a vice presidency. He just needs a little more gumption. I've dropped hints, but to no avail, which is why I took matters into my own hands.

"I got the name and home address of Bob's immediate boss, and, under the cloak of darkness, as they say, I drove over to the house and wired a tiny pipe bomb to the carburetor of their station car—you know, the junky car used to get husbands to and from the commuter train station. Theirs was a 1978 Volvo sedan. The kids were great and didn't make a peep while I installed the device. Bob was out pandering to some idiot client.

"Surprise, surprise, two weeks later, Bob stepped in and filled his old boss's shoes—actually, after the blast, they could only find one shoe. I hope Bob doesn't mess up, because I'll be very upset."

Nothing like the direct approach. Connie has decided to be less overtly aggressive. This type of woman is very dangerous, because it's nearly impossible to see past the fawning exterior to the sociopath seething inside. The lesson to be learned here is don't ever get in the way of a Beta.

Gamma Type

The Gamma type is easy to identify but difficult to control. She is capable of tweaking a man's most primal nerve. Basically a sniveler and whiner, the Gamma type is also very dangerous, because her obsequiousness can drive a good man crazy—sometimes to the point of murder, which works to her advantage. Whether she embodies great strength of character or plain old stupidity, the Gamma type keeps coming back for more. She even goes out of her way to award her mate's appropriate reactions.

1. _Interview 477-DK_

The comments below are from Dottie, a twenty-two-year-old systems analyst and the girlfriend of one of my patients. See if you can identify some of the Gamma characteristics.

"Harry's a wonderful boyfriend, so kind and considerate. Why, just the other day I made the foolish mistake of asking him if he could pick me up from work because my car was in the shop and I had to work past the time the buses stop running. After he pushed me into a large garbage bin by mistake, I realized just how pushy my request must have sounded. Why _shouldn't_ I hitch home? I mean, his time is just as valuable as mine. And how could I be so stupid as to forget that he'd already made plans to watch the rerun of last Sunday's exhibition scab football game with some of the guys? And who was going to prepare and serve the halftime seven-course meal?

"As soon as I'm out of the hospital and the dentist finishes my new bridge, I'm going to make it up to him. Maybe I'll cook his favorite Swedish meatballs, or wash and wax his Firebird, or . . ."

Pretty amazing, huh? This little lady is exhibiting some classic denial symptoms. See how obvious she is? Not only is her car in the shop, but she has to work late. What are those hungry lads going to eat between halves? In this situation and many like it, the Gamma ends up winning. How, you ask? Two ways. First, poor Harry lost face during the game because there was no food or beer (!) in the house (Dottie had conveniently neglected to do the shopping that day). Second, Harry lost so much weight during Dottie's one-week stay in the hospital he became delirious. He'd boasted that he'd never set foot inside a deli, or supermarket, or any place that sells uncooked food, and he refused to eat out, because Dottie was such a wonderful cook and he'd be damned if he'd pay money for a meal. So when next he visited Dottie in the hospital, he made the fateful error of asking her to marry him! Surprise, surprise. Who was the female manipulator who said, "The way to a man's heart is through his stomach"?

In discussing the incident with my patient, he realized that if it weren't for that fateful push he'd still be a single man. He'd also probably be fifty pounds lighter.

To add insult to injury, Dottie's dental problems kept her from giving those blow jobs he so richly deserved for a month after the accident. What a tragic story!

2. *Interview 019-HJ*

Arlene, a leggy, thirty-eight-year-old bee-keeper, is the crybaby girlfriend of my Ping-Pong partner. She's always calling him at the club to whine about one thing or another, invariably right at match point. Below is a conversation I got sucked into after my friend paid one of the club's staff members to pretend the call was from a patient of mine. I'll get you for that, Steve—you asshole.

"I've been stung so many times I can't tell you. Why can't I have a healthy relationship with a man? I love Steve, and I'd do anything for him, anything. Even though I'm usually busy as a bee, I'd drop everything if he wanted me to. Why, just the other day as we were walking down the street, Steve pointed out a tie he liked in the window of a fancy men's store. Well, later that day I rushed down to the store and bought the tie, a matching three-piece suit, and a nice cotton button-down shirt. But instead of being happy, he told me I was crazy. I guess he realizes a beekeeper doesn't make too much money. I apologized, and to make it up to him, I made reservations at a fancy French restaurant. But, again, he got angry with me.

"I don't understand it. My mother always told me you catch more flies with honey than with vinegar, but not in Steve's case. I like spending money on him, and I'd think nothing of taking out a second mortgage on my small one-bedroom co-op to buy a new compact disc player for him. My friends think I'm crazy, but they don't understand how much I love Steve. By the way, I have a bee in my bonnet, because I can't make up my mind: should I get plane tickets to Jamaica or the Virgin Islands? Don't tell Steve, because I want to surprise him. Oh, and can I borrow fifteen hundred dollars? I'll pay you back as soon as the check from the sale of my VW clears."

Pretty pathetic, huh? Well, think again. Arlene is a genius; she knows exactly what she's doing. It's the classic three-pronged approach—smother, guilt-trip, embarrass—perfected by the Gamma type, who slowly but surely gets her man.

First, she smothers him with love and adoration, something most men have a difficult time dealing with. Next, she gives him everything he desires, but she goes overboard, so he gets the sense that she can't control herself. Finally, she embarrasses the hell out of him—constantly crying on his friends' shoulders, borrowing huge sums of money, and contemplating suicide aloud in public places because she doesn't think he loves her. These insidious tactics are guaranteed to wear the poor guy down until he proposes. Why? Because the lasts thing he wants is to go through life feeling guilty. Little does he know that suicide is the furthest thing from her mind.

PART III

Coupling Couples

Now it's time to integrate the male and the female types. Introducing PIG, the Personality Interface Grid.

	Alpha	Beta	Gamma
Able	1	2	3
Baker	4	5	6
Charlie	7	8	9

This section examines each of the nine potential couplings and shows how the different types work together. Each combination describes a typical scenario and points out its various strengths and drawbacks. As an added attraction, I've included my own up-close-and-personal interviews with each of the men, for an unbiased impression of what this poor guys are going through. I think I changed the names to maintain a degree of anonymity, but I really can't remember.

COMBINATION #1:
ABLE TYPE MALE/
ALPHA TYPE FEMALE

The Scenario: Craig's favorite playthings are women and fast cars. Like most Able types, he believes vast differences exist between male and female roles and tries hard to maintain this state of affairs. Unfortunately for him, Craig hooked up with Jill, an Alpha type female.

Before they got married, BMOC Craig raced around in a fire-engine-red Camaro with Jill, the captain of the cheerleading squad, at his side. They were voted cutest couple in their senior class. Everything was fine until Jill got pregnant and they had to get married (they were devout—well, devout enough not to use rubbers—Catholics). As soon as that ring slid over the second knuckle on Jill's left hand, all hell broke loose. Jill had been hiding her predatory Alpha type tendencies behind the guise of a demure and fawning Gamma type. Imagine Craig's surprise.

After five tumultuous years of marriage, they worked out an interesting compromise: Jill was to concern herself with minor issues such as the family budget, how their savings should be invested, and their social life; Craig, in turn, was responsible for larger issues such as world disarmament, the ramifications of U.S. policy in Nicaragua, and whether UFOs are hallucinations or visible proof of intelligent life out there.

The Strengths: Able type men want to feel important and in control, which is why this relationship is a good example of symbiosis —look it up. Jill and Craig have managed to circumvent potential conflicts because each is in charge of specific, mutually exclusive aspects of their life together.

But wouldn't an Able type mind losing control over his money and his social life?

Of course, but most Able types have a very difficult time dealing with logic, especially female logic—and I use the term loosely—which renders them extremely susceptible to the wily machinations of the female mind. The Able type's vitality is centered in his strength of body, character, and conviction, evidenced by his selective memory and eventual ability to embrace almost any idea as his own.

As it stands, Craig is quite content spit-shining his Mustang GT—if Jill hasn't traded it in for a station wagon yet—while he figures out answers to today's more pressing worldly quandaries.

WARNING: The fairer sex realizes that men can't stand women who are threatening. More often than not, that purring Gamma kitten is really an Alpha tigress ready to pounce. The Able type male must be careful not to change into a Charlie type once he's nabbed. Make sure "important" doesn't become "impotent."

The Drawbacks: The Able type man experiences high levels of frustration with an Alpha type woman. Unlike Beta and Gamma women, the Alpha female goes toe to toe with her man, producing the best shouting matches around. This futility puts our Able type in a frustrating, no-win situation that could lead to terminal meltdown if the Alpha woman is not careful. Like the cornered animal, our Able male could easily strike out with a well-placed punch in the mouth if pushed too far. Unfortunately for the man, the Alpha woman is capable simultaneously of stopping short of getting her head bashed in while convincing him that her original position was really his own. I've observed this phenomenon many times, and it's not a pretty sight.

An Interview With Craig

EVANS: Craig, tell me a bit about your relationship with Jill.

CRAIG: What's to tell? Hey! Check out this new Hurst stick shift I picked up the other day with my allowance.

EVANS: Did you say "allowance," Craig?

CRAIG: No way, buddy! Who said anything about allowance? I can spend as much money as I want, you hear me?

EVANS: Sorry, Craig, I must've been mistaken.

CRAIG: That's okay, man. Just don't say that A word again.

EVANS: Sure. No problem.

CRAIG: Hey, did you know that on the night of January sixteenth, 1986, seven people in Ipswich, Massachusetts, reported a funny-looking aircraft hovering over a vacant lot? They said they saw strange flashing lights and heard what sounded like the theme song from "I Love Lucy."

EVANS: News to me, Craig.

CRAIG: Damn straight you didn't. The government's trying to cover it up.

EVANS: Craig, do you and Jill ever fight?

CRAIG: Hell, yes.

EVANS: Who usually wins?

CRAIG: I do, of course.

EVANS: Can you tell me what the most recent fight was about?

CRAIG: Sure. She wanted to go see *Rambo LVIII* and I wanted to go see *A Chorus Line*.

EVANS: That's interesting, Craig. I would have thought *Rambo* was more your kind of movie. I saw it the other day, and the special effects are great, especially the part where Stallone fries a bunch of Venusians with his trusty flamethrower.

CRAIG: Yeah, you're right. I must have just confused the two movies.

EVANS: Hmmmm, I can understand that. By the way, which movie did you go see?

CRAIG: *A Chorus Line.* I loved it.

COMBINATION #2
ABLE TYPE MALE/
BETA TYPE FEMALE

The Scenario: Our Able type, Dean, has traded his torn, sweat-stained Alcatraz Swim Team T-shirt for a torn, sweat-stained, teal green–locker room gray reversible sweatshirt that his Beta type wife, Liz, purchased for him from the J. Crew catalogue. It's sweat stained because Liz is too busy working part time at a friend's catering business to do the laundry. And since he's the Able type, he doesn't give a shit about the laundry, the shirt, etc.

But wait—wouldn't an Able type be the least likely to allow his wife to work? Not necessarily. Typically brighter than her Able type mate, the Beta woman has no problem convincing him that her salary will improve their life-style; they'll eat fancier dinners, for starters. Of course, Liz continues to feed him the usual dreck. In the event of a complaint, all she has to do is make reservations at the nearest Brew 'N' Burger, but odds are Dean will have forgotten the conversation by evening.

The Strengths: This Able type man is on to a good thing: a woman who'll work two or more jobs, keep the house presentable, and still be reasonably feminine. He's just not aware of the fact that he had very little to do with the arrangement. She's just being a competent modern woman, and in the long run, what he doesn't know won't hurt him.

The Drawbacks: Competition. The Able type male has a tendency to be threatened by his Beta wife. But remember, an industrious wife makes an Able type look good. Why struggle to keep up? While she's at aerobics class, the Able type can be having a few at the local bar. Think back to the Middle Ages, when womenfolk tilled the fields, birthed the young'uns, kept house, and made mead for the menfolk. Now *those* were manly days.

An Interview With Dean

EVANS: Dean, is it true you wear the pants in the family?

DEAN: Damn straight. In my house, I'm king.

EVANS: Does that mean you don't assume any any of the household duties, like doing the dishes or taking out the garbage?

DEAN: I wouldn't be caught dead doing that crap.

EVANS: Hmmm, interesting.

LIZ: [from the laundry room] Oh honey, would you show Mr. Evans how you make your muscles bulge when you fold the bed sheets?

DEAN: Aww, come on, Liz, he doesn't want to see my muscles.

EVANS: Oh, but I do. What a wonderful idea! I'd love to see the king of the castle fold the sheets.

DEAN: Well, all right.

[pause]

EVANS: Great job. There's quite a knack to folding those king-size fitted ones, isn't there? By the way, Dean, does it bother you that Liz has a job instead of staying at home like a typical housewife?

DEAN: Who are you kidding? She cooks fancy food for other people and gets paid for it. What a joke! That's not a real job.

EVANS: I see. Now, as I understand it, you make fifteen dollars an hour as a riveter for an independent construction company, while Liz makes approximately one thousand dollars per catering event. She spends about twenty hours per event, including preparation and service. Less, say, about two hundred dollars for food. If my math is correct, that comes to forty dollars an hour. Does it bother you that your wife—

LIZ: Ah, Dean, Dean honey, look what time it is! Isn't the Seahawks game on now?

DEAN: Thanks Lizzie. I got to go, Evans. I'll be back at halftime.

LIZ: You climb into your special La-Z-Boy football chair, dear, and I'll bring you a Schlitz and a bowl of Cheez Doodles in just a second. [pause] That was close! Listen, asshole, promise me this instant no more questions about who makes more money or I scream rape.

EVANS: Sure, Liz. Let's not do anything rash. In fact, it might be best if I just leave.

LIZ: I think that's a very good idea.

COMBINATION #3:
ABLE TYPE MALE/
GAMMA TYPE FEMALE

The Scenario: Speed (his real name's Macon) oversees the world's oldest profession: he's a purveyor of human flesh, a manager of delectable meat, a pimp. His stable includes three lovely ladies of the night, Trudy, Angel, and Baby, to whom he refers as his "family."

A tough entrepreneur, Speed makes it a point to keep his assets in line. He's also an

Able type. Trudy, Angel, and Baby are scared to death of his terrible mean streak. He demands quite a bit from his employees/family and if anyone fails to meet her quota, he's been known to carve his initials on a tender piece of flesh.

Like many Able types, Speed wants total control over the women in his life. Much of this need stems from a childhood spent with an overbearing, rather strict mother, the type who punished her children by locking them in an old refrigerator for an hour or so, or chaining them to the bed while she went off to work. I guess it's a very fine line between control and hatred of the female of the species.

Let's face it, most Able type men who seek Gamma women are making a rather obvious statement. These guys want to get back at their mothers, who in turn were getting back at their husbands or fathers, who in turn . . . and on and on and on. The bottom line is that these guys are angry and they want their day in the sun. No matter what Trudy, Angel, and Baby were before they met Speed, they're all Gamma types now.

The Strengths: Speed is his own man, and to hell with anyone who thinks otherwise —and that includes those "dumb bitches" (his words). Via intimidation and drugs, Speed has created a comfortable little home and business for himself in the drug-infested projects of downtown Detroit. There's no question who's in charge, which has eliminated a potential source of much strife.

The Drawbacks: Watch your back, Jack. As I mentioned earlier, Gamma types—even converts—are insidious. They don't get mad, they get even. They'll make you so angry you'll end up doing something stupid, and that could spell financial ruin for someone like Speed. He could lose 33 percent of his business if he has to take one of his ladies off the street and rearrange her face because she was silly enough to embezzle a few bucks.

From the Able type's point of view, the major drawback is his anger, because it usually gets him in a shitload of trouble. Unfortunately, the Gamma is the perfect type to bring this out. Poor Speed has his hands full worrying about competition, narcs, rip-offs, and bad product. The last thing he needs to fret about is a murder-one rap when he offs one of his ladies because she got him a little riled.

Note: Able-Gamma relationships go through more body bags than garbage bags—all to the detriment of the male, who usually has to stand trial. Miserably, provocation isn't one of the better defenses.

An Interview With Speed

EVANS: So, Mr. Speed, tell me a little about yourself.

SPEED: I'm lean, I'm mean, I'm a money-makin' machine. I'm takin' my piece of the pie and dat ain't no lie.

EVANS: Tell me a little bit about your "extended family," Mr. Speed.

SPEED: Say what?

EVANS: Uh, clue me into your babe trade.

SPEED: Oh, you want to know how me and my sweeties get along? Well, it be like flies to honey. Ain't that right, sugar? Don't you be looking at my face, bitch [slap]. Next time I be knocking out your front toof.

EVANS: So, Mr. Speed, would you say you have a healthy relationship with these three women?

SPEED: Yo, honkie, deese girls be clean. You ain't gonna find no clap or AIDS shit with my sweeties. They be A-One prime beef on the hoof.

EVANS: I don't doubt that for a second, Mr. Speed.

SPEED: Why you be axing me all deese questions? You be vice or sumpin'? Hey, what da hell is dis? Is you wired?

EVANS: No, no, Mr. Speed. That's nothing but a—Wait! Don't pull th—

COMBINATION #4:
BAKER TYPE MALE/
ALPHA TYPE FEMALE

The Scenario: Intelligent and thorough, formerly a loan officer at County Savings and Loan, Baker type Matthew has given up his job to stay home and watch the kids. At first glance, this behavior might be confused with that of the Charlie type, especially when the individual in question has hooked up with an Alpha female. But instead of cringing, the Baker type relies on his illusion of self-assurance to defend against her onslaughts. For example, when his wife, Susan, asked him what he thought about the '90s male, Matthew was quick to brag that he and others of his ilk were unthreatened by the new positions held by women in business. Unfortunately, he went on to praise the new family dynamic, where the man stays home and the wife continues to work. Before you could say "What the fuck?" poor Matthew was wearing an apron and washing out the baby bottles, while Susan went on with her job as a stewardess for a major airline.

Now Matthew cleans house, cooks the meals, does the laundry, and picks up the kids after school. He also makes a mean bundt cake (the secret is real vanilla beans and to let it cool in a warm place) and hasn't missed one Oprah or Phil Donahue show since he's changed jobs. Last week, Matthew won the Phoenix Jaycee's Best House-person Award for the second year in a row

The Strengths: Baker type men have a resilient smugness about them that allows them to rationalize virtually any situation, even those not in their favor. This clouds their thinking and allows them to embrace their new roles with a vengeance. It also appeases their guilt at not trying to differentiate between male and female roles.

The Drawbacks: See Strengths.

An Interview With Matthew

EVANS: So, Matthew, how do you like being a househusband?

MATTHEW: I like it very much. By the way, I much prefer being referred to as a domestic engineer.

EVANS: Excuse me. Matthew, how did you and your wife decide who was going to keep working and who was going to do the housework?

MATTHEW: I assume when you say "housework," you mean home management?

EVANS: Of course.

MATTHEW: Well, I'm not really sure. It couldn't have been the money, because I was making more. Hmmm. It wasn't who had the better job, because I was in line for a vice presidency and Susan has at least fifteen more years before she earns seniority and rates free tickets to Epcot Center and Disney World. Oh, *I* remember. Susan said that since I'm so sure of my own masculinity, I was one of the only men she knew who could deal with this role reversal. She also said that in my heart of hearts I wanted to prove it, so that's why I would have volunteered if she hadn't already made the decision for us. See?

EVANS: In a slightly roundabout way, yes. It's great to see how comfortable you are with your new role as domestic engineer and—

CHILDREN: [from the TV room] We're hungry. When are you going to be done talking? We want our tuna melts and Jell-O pops!

MATTHEW: We're just about done. Mommy will be right there.

EVANS: Matthew, do you realize you just said "Mommy"?

MATTHEW: What? Are you kidding? Ha, ha. How silly. I wonder what good old Sigmund would say about that? Ha, ha, ha. Are you sure?

COMBINATION #5:
BAKER TYPE MALE/
BETA TYPE FEMALE

The Scenario: Bob and Marsha are both thirty-seven, and they've been married for a little over three months. Both are on the fast track; Bob's in commercial real estate and Marsha, an obvious Beta type, is an account supervisor at a major public relations firm. They work long hours and seldom get to see each other, so the time they do spend together is considered "quality time."

Bob married Marsha because she seemed to embody many of the characteristics he valued in himself: a sense of purpose, intelligence, independence (she kept her own name), a moderate sense of humor, and a burning desire to succeed in business. Little did he know. Marsha's hidden agenda surfaced once the marriage contract was signed—she wanted children and she wanted them now. One month after they were married, Marsha was pregnant. And Bob's reaction? He can't wait to be a daddy.

What happened? Marsha realized that under Bob's Baker type veneer lay the soul of a macho man who craved immortality. This could only be achieved by siring a generation of little Bobs. Bob could do Marsha's bidding—and like it! Marsha's no fool. She—I mean they—won't decide whether she'll go back to work until she checks out how much work is involved in raising a child.

The only problem: Marsha better have a boy. She'll probably manage that, too. If not, of course she'll manage to convince Bob that every real man needs a daughter to worship him.

The Strengths: The Baker type is the most open to change—albeit, not on a conscious level. He is also relaxed with a woman who is just as successful and independent as he.

Finally, he is unaware of the threat many women pose to his way of thinking.

The Drawbacks: The Baker type is very fragile, because he's caught between his desires to be an animal concerned only with survival of the fittest and his guilty desire to be a sensitive, caring male of the Nineties. Women of all types know this and take full advantage.

An Interview With Bob

EVANS: Bob, congratulations! I understand you're going to be a father.

BOB: Yeah, and I can't wait. A Bob, Jr., to carry on the line.

EVANS: Looking at your questionnaire, I noticed that you don't seem to be threatened by working women who compete with you in the business environment. Does that egalitarianism extend to relationships, too?

BOB: It sure does. I'll never forget the way my mother was taken advantage of by my father. She'd slave all day keeping the house clean, making the meals, watching us kids, doing the shopping . . . you know, all that mom/homemaker stuff. And my dad didn't appreciate any of it. You know how it goes: no paycheck, no respect.

EVANS: I don't understand what this has to do with working women.

BOB: Well, I believe it's time women had a chance to choose careers other than that of a housewife.

EVANS: But now you and your wife are expecting a baby. Is she going to stay home and take care of the child or go back to work?

BOB: Jesus, that's a good question. We haven't discussed that yet.

EVANS: If you could write the script, what would you choose?

BOB: I don't really know. I guess a child should have his mother around, but why should the mother be saddled with child care? Then again, I wouldn't want a stranger bringing up my heir and namesake. I just don't know. I think I'm getting a headache.

EVANS: Okay, Bob, just one more question. What happens if Marsha has a girl?

BOB: Marsha! Where's the Librium?

COMBINATION #6:
BAKER TYPE MALE/
GAMMA TYPE FEMALE

The Scenario: Barry is the East Asian ceramics buyer for a major auction house in New York City, specializing in Sung dynasty porcelain. He is married to Mei-ling, a Chinese woman he met while tracking down fifteenth-century clay figurines from the tomb of an obscure mandarin in Xi'an, China. Mei-ling stays home, takes care of Barry's two children from a previous marriage, and keeps the apartment clean. Barry and Mei-ling have a good relationship; Barry is the master and Mei-ling is the help. That may sound a bit crass, but both parties are more than satisfied with the arrangement.

It's obvious why Barry has no problem with the setup, and if you're familiar with the Asian mentality, you understand why it suits Mei-ling, too. Women in China are treated as second-class citizens. Thankful that her new American husband won't throw her out on the street for burning the rice, Mei-ling lives to be stepped on. And this is a perfect example of the relationship between a Baker type male and a Gamma type female.

There is a difference between the Baker type male and his Able type counterpart. Instead of trying to break in a ball-busting East Coast feminist, Barry looked to the Far East, choosing a woman from an overtly male-dominated culture. Obsequious Mei-ling just bows and makes the beds.

Better yet, Barry is considered sensitive, debonair, and worldly; his knowledgeable friends know it's inappropriate to force someone from a foreign culture to jettison her own customs.

The Strengths: Barry is at one with his type. Instead of rationalizing and justifying, like most Baker types, this one has learned to use his natural proclivities to his advantage.

The Drawbacks: The Baker type has a very narrow "window of happiness." The only type that won't either walk all over him or abuse his sensitivity is a woman from a female-oppressed culture. And hooking up with someone from the Third World does have its disadvantages: the language barrier, weird food, silly shoes, and strange religious rites, just to name a few. Baker types in this situation admit that intellectual conversation is sometimes lacking, and it's especially hard to maintain one when your wife's walking six feet behind you.

CAUTION: These women can be much more insidious, controlling, and inscrutable than the worst Western Gamma types. I've heard stories of angry Chinese woman poisoning their husbands, and then there's the Japanese woman who was so jealous, she cut off her unfaithful lover's balls when he was asleep. Ouch! So exercise extreme care.

Note: The Baker type man needs a woman who'll understand him and tell him how he should understand himself.

Interview With Barry

EVANS: Barry, why did you marry an Oriental?

BARRY: I guess the best answer to that question, Mr. Evans, is that she was the first woman whom I really felt comfortable with and who understood me.

EVANS: But isn't it true that she doesn't know a word of English?

BARRY: Not at all. She knows, "please," "thank you," "Mr. Clean," "spin cycle," "Ziploc bag," "please forgive clumsy self." Anyway, our relationship transcends verbal expression. Excuse me for a second. We should have had our tea by now. [*clap, clap*] Ah, there you are, Mei-ling. Where is our tea? You know I have a guest. [pause] Tea, *tea*. Cha.

MEI-LING: So solly. Wood wet. Fire not start.

BARRY: Mei-ling, how many times do I have to tell you? Use the stove. You know, big square firebox. Turn black knob, put kettle on fire.

MEI-LING: So solly. Mei-ling very stupid.

	Bally would like to beat disglaceful wife?
BARRY:	Not now—I mean no, no dear. I'm not mad, just make the tea. Our guest is thirsty and so am I. And when you're done, go get my shirts from the cleaner.
MEI-LING:	Yes, my master, your humble servant hears and obeys.
BARRY:	Ha, ha. Ah, Mei-ling, don't say "servant."
MEI-LING:	But master—
BARRY:	*Mei-ling*, don't say "master," either.
MEI-LING:	But, sir—
BARRY:	That will be enough. You may go now. Ha, ha. . . . Well, Mr. Evans, you can take the girl out of China, but you can't take China out of the girl.
EVANS:	Yeah, Barry, I can see what you're up against.

COMBINATION #7: CHARLIE TYPE MALE/ ALPHA TYPE FEMALE

The Scenario: Jeremy has been living with Beth for a year and a half. Unfortunately, Jeremy is a Charlie type in a relationship with an Alpha type female. He didn't realize two-hundred-fifty-pound, five-foot-two-inch Beth was moving in until she appeared at his door early one Saturday morning with a steamer trunk, a crate of cookbooks, and a gross of Hostess cupcakes. Jeremy had met Beth two days earlier at a Weight Watchers meeting. (He's far from overweight, but a well-meaning friend had suggested it as a likely place to meet a nice, wretched girl who'd put out.)

More forward than desperate, Beth decided that she and Jeremy would make a great couple. They were married two weeks later. Poor Jeremy was the last to know.

Typical of the Charlie type, Jeremy allowed Beth to steamroll him. Instead of confronting the issues, he decided to stay out of the house as much as possible. On top of his job at the public library, Jeremy worked at an all-night bookstore, only going home to sleep, shower, and change. Adding to the insult, if Beth happened to be home at one of the odd times that Jeremy showed up, she forced him to cook complicated meals like coq au vin, beef Wellington, and tandoori chicken by threatening to sit on his cat, Sinbad.

The Strengths: I can't think of any.

The Weaknesses: A Charlie type male should never go out with an Alpha type female—unless he's a masochist. The Alpha women love to get their hands on Charlie type men so they can wreak retribution on every man in their lives who did them wrong. And why not? The Charlie type male is the perfect whipping boy.

An Interview With Jeremy

EVANS: Jeremy, thank you for seeing me and I'm sorry if I came at an inopportune time. . . . I thought you said Beth wasn't going to be home.

BETH: Oh, I wouldn't have missed this for the world. I just want to make sure

that Jeremy has his facts straight.
The man can be so scatterbrained
sometimes.

JEREMY: But why would I lie?

BETH: Quiet, dear, and let Mr. Evans ask
his questions.

JEREMY: Okay.

EVANS: Jeremy, tell me a little bit about your
relationship with Beth.

JEREMY: Well—

BETH: Oh, let me answer that one. Jeremy
and I met at the opening of Pucci-
ni's *Madame Butterfly* at Lincoln
Center. I was wearing a black and
gold strapless de la Renta taffeta
evening gown. I was surrounded
by a group of tall, handsome men
in Armani tuxedos—you know,
with the dropped shoulders—

EVANS: Excuse me, Beth, but Jeremy told
me he met you at a Weight Watchers meeting.

BETH: [*smack*] Jeremy, if I've told you once,
I've told you a thousand times, I
can't abide lying.

JEREMY: Ouch. But we really did—

BETH: [*smack*] Hush, sweetie. Next question, please.

EVANS: Jeremy, if you could sum up your relationship in one word, what would that word be?

BETH: Blissful. Isn't that right?

JEREMY: Ah, well . . . [smack] Ouch! Yes!

EVANS: Beth, I get the feeling Jeremy isn't really telling me his side of the story.

BETH: Well, you're wrong. I don't dominate you, do I honey? Well, Jeremy?

JEREMY: Ah . . . [smack] Ow!

EVANS: I'm sorry, Beth, but I really must tell you that your behavior is atrocious.

JEREMY: No, please, don't say that! She's fine. There's no problem.

BETH: You heard him, Mr. Fancy Pants, there's no problem. How dare you come into my house and try to cause friction between my husband and me. Take that! [smack]

EVANS: Ouch!

JEREMY: Honey, I don't think—[smack] Ow!

BETH: And that! [smack]

EVANS: Ow! That hurt!

BETH: And here's one for you. [smack]

JEREMY: Ouch!

BETH: I'm not through with you, yet, Mr. Interviewer. [*smack*]

EVANS: Ouch!

BETH: Give me that stupid tape recor—

COMBINATION #8:
CHARLIE TYPE MALE/
BETA TYPE FEMALE

The Scenario: A clown on the South Texas rodeo circuit, Steve spends most of his afternoons and evenings jumping in and out of large rubber barrels so as to avoid being mauled or trampled by bucking broncs and angry bulls. Steve is married to Joan, a claims adjustor for a large Southwestern life insurance company. Believe it or not, Steve is a Charlie type male. Before Steve met Joan, he'd been a math teacher at an all-girls school. Insecure and bored, Steve was wasting away in a job that had lost its luster ten years earlier. One day, Joan, the mother of one of his students, walked into his classroom to pick up her daughter, and it was love at first sight.

Steve's life changed because Joan was willing to push him into areas that challenged and stimulated both his mind and his body. Joan was good at this kind of cheerleading, because she'd done it twice before. Unfortunately, both of her previous husbands experienced untimely deaths; number one from injuries sustained at the claws of a lion he was trying to convince to jump through a flaming hoop, number two disemboweled by an angry bull in the middle of a Mexican bullring, to the delight of the crowd. Luckily, Joan had taken out healthy coverage on both and was able to assuage her sorrow with large cash settlements.

Call it coincidence, but both of Joan's previous husbands were not only stuck in dead-end jobs—number one was a librarian and number two a professional dog walker—they were both Charlie types!

The Strengths: There is no artifice or hidden agenda about the Charlie type. They are loyal, kind, and courteous, much like a Boy Scout or a well-trained house pet. Charlie types are open to change because they've nowhere to go but up.

The Drawbacks: In the hands of the wrong woman, our Charlie type can be so much putty. Unlike the relatively blatant Alpha type, the Beta type female is more insidious and, for anyone other than a Charlie type male, more difficult to spot. His knowledge won't help him, though, because he'll still be used and abused.

An Interview With Steve

EVANS: Steve, you made quite a career change, from the staid life of a high school math teacher to the rather dangerous occupation of rodeo clown. Can you explain the drastic switch?

STEVE: It's as much as a surprise to me as it is to you, Mr. Evans.

[pause]

EVANS: So that's it? Don't you have any feelings on how this change has affected your life?

STEVE: Wait a minute. Joan knew this question might come up and so she jotted down a few ideas she thought might help me. Hold on. [pause] Yeah, here it is. "Steve, tell the nice man that

the greatest change in your life has
been marriage to a woman like me."

[pause]

EVANS: Okay, tell me about Joan.

STEVE: Hang on a sec. [pause] "Tell the man
that I'm a simple, kind, and understanding wife. You might also mention my infectious love of animals and
my expertise as a life insurance bro-
ker. Ask him what kind of coverage
does he have? We offer a superlative
'accidental death and dismember-
ment' plan."

[pause]

EVANS: I'll be glad to discuss my insurance
situation with Joan, Steve. But tell
me, how do you feel about all this?

STEVE: [pause] I feel . . . ah, I feel . . . "Steve,
tell him you feel lucky to have found
a devoted wife who only wants the
best for her man. Tell him that you're
thinking of getting rid of that stupid
safety helmet you wear while waiting for the wild bronco to kick the
barrel you're sitting in, because it de-
tracts from the realism." Oh, my, I
don't know. [pause] "Just read the
answers, honey."

EVANS: Steve, sounds to me like Joan's doing most of the talking, and she's not even here. Can you put down those papers for a minute and give me a straight answer?

[pause]

STEVE: Hmmm . . . [pause] "How dare you talk to my husband that way. I think it's time for you to leave. Say goodbye to the man, Steve." [pause] Goodbye, Mr. Evans.

COMBINATION #9:
CHARLIE TYPE MALE/
GAMMA TYPE FEMALE

The Scenario: Ron works in a subway token booth, which is how he met his girlfriend, Sandy—Ron's pet name for her—a diagnosed paranoid schizophrenic who lives in the bowels of New York's West Side IRT. Sandy had been in Bellevue, but escaped when she found out they were trying to assassinate her for causing the greenhouse effect, the hole in the ozone layer, and the nomination of Dan Quayle. By her own admission, Sandy is unsure whether the first two claims are justifiable, but vehemently denies any link whatsoever to the last one.

Ron and Sandy have an interesting relationship. She thinks Ron is the Mind-Control Commander of an alien space force that's using the subway token booths to relay messages about Sandy's whereabouts to the mother ship; Ron, who chose the safe confines of a token booth because he's deathly afraid of people in general and women in particular, has finally found someone who repects him. Ron is so into his role that he now sports an old plastic Steve Canyon Jet Helmet. Sandy, on the other hand, is so far gone I'm not certain which role she's playing.

Ron and Sandy are a good example of how a Charlie type and a Gamma type can get along together. They both derive comfort from their fantasy lives. And why not? Remember: any kind of lovin' is good lovin', even though it may be a mite fucked up and weird.

The Strengths: A very vivid imagination or a liberal sprinkling of psychosis.

The Weaknesses: Reality.

An Interview With Ron

EVANS: Ron, wouldn't you say your relationship with Sandy is pretty unique?

RON: [*crackle*] Hmmf ritff grust. [*crackle*]

EVANS: I'm sorry, Ron, I can't understand you when you're speaking through that authentic-looking Steve Canyon Jet Helmet's strap-on mouthpiece.

RON: Ooops. I forget I have it on sometimes. People often tell me I sound like the audio address system down here when I'm wearing this thing. What was the question?

EVANS: I just commented that your relationship with Sandy is somewhat unique.

RON: Sure is. I really love that girl. She's the first woman I've ever gone out with who really likes me for *me*.

EVANS: That's great, Ron. Tell me, what's a typical date for you two?

RON: *Date?!* I try not to leave the token booth unless I have to, and in any case, Sandy is too paranoid to let me get near her. It works out best this way, especially since Sandy doesn't believe in taking a bath. She says water burns her skin like battery acid.

EVANS: You know that that's pretty strange, don't you?

RON: Sure I do, but this is how we like it. You see, she thinks if she looks at me directly—you know, without this leaded-glass shield—she'll melt. *What* an imagination. I, on the other hand, revert to a mass of quivering jelly outside this booth.

EVANS: Are you satisfied? I mean, it doesn't sound like the relationship's going anywhere.

RON: Probably not, but what're you going to do? Hey, there's Sandy now.

SANDY: [from the middle of the subway tracks] Hail, Supreme Ruler of the Nether World and Commander of Alien Life Forms. Just wait until the innocent oxygen breathers of Earth hear about your malevolent plot to take control. I'll get the message out; you can't stop me.

RON: Excuse me. [*crackle*] Krunk brucnk hurrunk sjeyfhd dhfutiw ehwjhfh djfsdj xbzuam! [*crackle*] Sorry, she

doesn't take me seriously unless I
put on the helmet.

EVANS: Wow! Look at her run!

RON: I'd put her up against Flo-Jo any day.

CONCLUSION

By now you should have an idea of where
you fit on the male spectrum and what you
should expect in the way of female com-
panionship.

The common denominator transcends all
male types: forget about the strengths each
type brings to a relationship, because men
are just quivering protoplasm in the hands
of their women. Kick and scream, rationalize and relate, or whimper and cringe; it's
not going to change. The saying "A guy's
gotta do what a guy's gotta do" only works
in Rambo and John Wayne movies; the reality is, "A guy's gotta do what a guy's gotta
do, if it's all right with the little woman."

Don't despair! There's still hope, because
wherever you find yourself, hundreds of
hungry women are waiting, more than willing to accommodate your idiosyncrasies in

exchange for a wedding ring, or even just a steady date on Saturday nights. But beware of losing that all-important marketing advantage. Remember, as soon as you settle down you've had it, you've lost your edge. When does this occur? Sometime between the third date and moving in together; I can't put my finger on the exact time, unfortunately. Hell, if I could, I'd be a millionaire by now. For now, all I can say is watch your back!

Sorry to be such a downer. I don't know about you, but I'm really depressed. What do you say we move along to Part IV?

PART IV

Can My Type Be Edited?

Let's say you're not satisfied with your type and think matters can be improved. Say you're a Baker type guy, but you'd like to take matters into your own hands and become more of an Able type, or you're a Charlie type who got lucky dodging a punch from his wife and feels it's time to assert himself. Or perhaps you're an Able type who's fed up with all the fierce competition, frustration, and lack of nuance your role demands and you would prefer the more covert, smug, Baker type approach.

This chapter will show you how.

Note: In order to change your type, you must modify many of your habits, and not just those that relate to women. What you wear, how you present yourself, your occupation, your home life, as well as your relationship to your fellow man are some of the important factors that may be involved. There must be others, but I can't think of them right now.

<u>Oh Yeah, Another Note:</u> If you decide to change your type, you have to change completely. For example, you get no credit if you're sporting a white crew-neck Fruit of the Loom undershirt, faded Levi's jeans, white athletic socks, and Tony Lama cowboy boots but still work as a fact checker for *Gourmet* magazine.

On the other hand, no points will be awarded if you slave over a cake for your wife's birthday while knocking back shots of bourbon. I guarantee when she arrives home and finds a slobbering mess ruining her kitchen, she'll kill you. To be consistent with the sensitive chef role, you must take tiny sips of some cheap Chablis or cooking sherry and stop when your cheeks feel flush.

CHANGING FROM ABLE
TO BAKER

Pissed that your old lady is pulling a fast one on you and you can't figure out how she's doing it? Is it increasingly difficult to stir up the energy to slap the little woman around when she's being a pain in the ass? Have you discovered that yelling, "Yo, chickie babe, wanna fuck?" to a woman on the street isn't the best of come-ons? Smooth those rather rough edges by following the advice below, and become a man women can talk to—and then go down on.

<u>Note</u>: Becoming a Baker type will not help you understand women better. But it will improve your ability to rationalize the situation and convince yourself it really isn't that important.

CLOTHING

Informal
• Be a tad more fastidious. For example, try not to wear your underwear more than two days in a row, and use a Kleenex instead of your shirt sleeve.

- Wear more colors (maroons, dark green, ochres, and terra-cottas, *not* pastels), but get rid of anything in locker-room gray, jock blue, or athlete's-foot red. Any type of pullover in cotton with short sleeves and a collar will do—you know, stuff like Polo or Lacoste. WARNING: Don't use the shirt to make a fashion statement. Never wear your collar up because most men who do are real assholes. Trust me on this one; I've done studies.
- Stop wearing anything with a number emblazoned on the front.
- Trade in some of your faded blue jeans for corduroys and chinos.

Formal
- Start wearing clothes that match. (That means stop walking around looking like a test pattern. The key phrase here: dress to impress.)
- Pick up some pants that have creases. Keep them creased. Do *not* iron your jeans. Buy an iron but feign confusion when your wife/ girlfriend explains how it works.
- Familiarize yourself with the local dry cleaners.

- Purchase shirts with buttons that go *all* the way down the front.
- Buy ties (the kind you tie yourself).
- Stock up on shoes that can be polished. Stock up on shoe polish, too. Don't let your friends catch her polishing your shoes—that's a man's job. (Though it's okay if she does it in private.)
- Wear ascots and dinner jackets to all parties serving food.
- Buy a black tuxedo and never rent one again.
- Put monograms on all your business shirts. Request monogrammed handkerchiefs—never call them "hankies"—as a gift from someone you want to impress.

PERSONAL HABITS

- Start showering daily.
- Shaving is a must. You must be sensitive to the irritation the rubbing of a prickly mustache or beard can cause to a woman's creamy soft skin.
- You can still sit on the porcelain throne each morning for twenty minutes or so, but don't groan in ecstasy as much, and

start working on crossword puzzles or the *Reader's Digest* "Enrich Your Vocabulary" quiz.

- Stop asking your wife/girlfriend/female acquaintance to pull your thumb, farting loudly when she obliges.
- Sit up straight.
- Don't talk with your mouth full.
- Eat all your peas.

RELATIONS WITH WOMEN

- Count to ten before you tell a woman she's full of shit.
- Practice complimenting her; it makes no difference whether or not you're sincere.
- Take your date to fewer sporting events and more movies with subtitles. If this means glasses, that's okay. Women *like* glasses, especially horn-rims, because they make the wearer look smarter than he really is.
- Don't expect much in the area of sports knowledge. For example, don't get pissed if she thinks the Boston Celtics are an Irish singing group. And be tolerant if she confuses a bunt with a bogie. <u>Note</u>: Do not expect a woman—any woman—to con-

sider a *Sports Illustrated* subscription a romantic gift.

- The only sports you should share with a woman are croquet, badminton, or bridge. This way if she beats you, none of your male friends will give a shit.
- Pretend to listen.
- Nod knowingly when she starts to talk about "feelings" and "emotions," even if you don't care or can't follow.
- Check out the Terms section in the back of this book for some of the appropriate psychobabble in current use.
- Always agree, even if she says something fucked up and weird about your mother or your arrested development. Subterfuge is the name of the game. Don't get mad, get even. Switch the subject and say something like, "Honey, is that pimple still on the tip of your nose?"
- Learn to cry in front of her. Onion juice may help.

RELATIONS WITH MEN

- When greeting a friend, don't hit him in the arm anymore, and start saying "ouch" when he hits you.

- Instead of guys night out at the local saloon, racetrack, porno flick, or bowling alley, spend more time with mixed couples. (Don't worry, the women will arrange the details.)
- In fact, spend less time with your friends. They're a bad influence.

OCCUPATION

- Switch from a blue-collar to a white-collar job. If you already have a white-collar job, start scheming for a promotion, or switch companies, taking valuable accounts with you.
- Start a car pool.
- Buy a briefcase. Leather. No Nauga or vinyl crap.
- See Clothing: Formal.

HOME LIFE

- Learn to empty the garbage and dry the dishes.
- Stop referring to salt and pepper as "spices."
- Eat foods with strange-sounding names; use chopsticks.
- Watch CNN instead of ESPN.

- Drink martinis instead of beer. If you must drink beer, drink imported.

GENERAL ATTITUDE

- Be sensitive.
- Be understanding.
- Be caring.
- Be less physical.
- Be a woman's pal.
- Be able to tell what PMS stands for.
- Be a do bee, don't be a don't bee.
- Scooby dooby doo.

CHANGING FROM BAKER TO ABLE

Are you uncertain whether you should "agree to disagree" or just tell the bitch to "eat shit and die"? Would you rather putter around the garden or putt for par on the golf course? Have you had it up to here with couples therapy, feminist seminars, and vasectomy chat? Have you been thinking more and more often how great it would be to let loose and leave your wife at home while you go to a hockey game with the guys?

If you're a Baker type and have been plagued by one or more of these questions, you're a candidate for Able type status. To complete the picture, follow these instructions:

CLOTHING

Informal
- Wearing a T-shirt? Rip it.
- Tear the sleeves off all of your shirts.
- Buy shirts with numbers on them.
- Lose your shoelaces, or just never tie them.
- Wear your gym clothes outside of the gym.
- Never wear anything that's ironed.
- Let your woman shop for you, but make sure she only patronizes sporting goods or outdoorsmen stores.
- Get a black leather jacket with lots of hardware on it.
- Don't wear socks. If you must, make sure they're white tube socks.
- Wear heavy construction boots all year round.
- Only wear baseball caps with the names of heavy equipment companies embla-

zoned across the top (e.g., Deere, Caterpillar).

Formal
- If working in a high-level job where looks matter (e.g., stockbroker, company president, tycoon), dress to intimidate (e.g., power ties, power suits, power shoes, power saw).
- All other times, see Informal.

PERSONAL HABITS

- Burp and fart within female earshot. Smile and repeat louder when she expresses scorn.
- Sweat more. Deodorant is taboo. Only Old Spice or English Leather are permissible, if you *must* use perfume.
- Don't waste valuable time bathing, shaving, brushing your teeth, etc.
- Develop dandruff. Don't treat it.
- Get rid of all your handkerchiefs and start using your sleeve. Practice snot-flinging.

RELATIONS WITH WOMEN

- When making a date, sound uninterested.
- Cancel dates at the last minute without giving any excuse.

- Example of a typical date: insist on dinner at her place; bring some beer and drink it all; don't help clean up.
- Blame all misunderstandings on her.
- When in doubt, threaten her verbally. Then physically.
- Replace the word *woman* with *bimbo*.
- Stop being understanding. Don't worry; soon it'll be second nature.
- Look dumb when the topic of feelings or commitment comes up. If she persists, buy her Barry Manilow's Greatest Hits: "Feelings, nothing more than feelings . . ."

RELATIONS WITH MEN

- Spend more of your evenings drinking beer, watching the tube, and scratching your belly. If these activities bore you, pick up the latest issue of *Playboy* or *Penthouse* and snort and slobber at the centerfold while your wife is in the room.
- Go to more Clint Eastwood film festivals, Rambo movies, and anything starring Schwarzenegger.
- Hang out at the gym more often. If you're not the athletic type, learn to play pool.

- Get sloppy drunk and practice puking on your shoes.
- Frequent bars with Irish names.
- If a friend starts talking about troubles at home, recommend he see a therapist, then snicker condescendingly.
- If he *still* bugs you about his family problems, buy him shots of tequila until he shuts up or passes out, whichever comes first.
- Say "fuckin' A" a lot.

OCCUPATION

- Find a job in which ordinary soap won't get your hands clean after a day's work. Or work in an office where all the women are called girls.
- Refuse to work for a woman under any circumstances. If unavoidable, try to get into her panties. If unsuccessful, insult her femininity and spread lewd rumors about her in the men's room.
- If a woman makes more money than you, jump her in the parking lot.
- Make all your important contacts at all-male athletic clubs. Hurry before the new laws come into effect.

HOME LIFE

- Stop cleaning up messes.
- Start making more messes.
- Let your woman make all the social plans, but refuse to go along with them if you have to change your clothes, wear a tie after working hours, or drink beer out of a glass.
- Never go into the kitchen, unless it's to the fridge for a brewski. If you have kids, train them to get the beer for you as soon as they can walk.
- Start having all-night poker games and invite at least one friend who smokes cigars.
- Forget all special dates, like your wife's birthday and your anniversary.
- Put your feet up on all the furniture.
- Insist on a large, hairy dog to keep her safe while you're out drinking. Don't walk it.
- Trade in your wimpy Japanese-built car for a Jeep Wagoneer from the good ol' U.S. of A. Accessorize with sheepskin seat covers and a gun rack.

GENERAL ATTITUDE

- Be gruff.
- Be inconsiderate.

- Be in control.
- Be slightly dim.
- Be sick of things like "emotions," "feelings," etc.
- Be physical.

CHANGING FROM CHARLIE TO ABLE

This is the most difficult of all, and virtually impossible if the person plans to remain with the same woman, in the same town, or on the same job. Let's face it, who's going to believe a guy who's physically intimidated by his own wife is capable of defending himself, let alone self-assertion.

But once you've left your woman, moved to another state, and possibly undergone facial surgery, you should be able to effect the change without too much difficulty. Remember, you're a Charlie type by nature and must be forever on your guard not to reveal it, or you're lost. Here's a helpful hint so you don't revert by mistake: as soon as you've established yourself in your new surroundings, get a tattoo of a skull and crossbones on your arm or somewhere more visible, like the back of your hand. Granted it sounds a bit drastic, but you're going to need all the help you can get. And do what it says below—now!

CLOTHING

Informal

- Some of you are halfway there, especially if you're married to a woman who likes to throw you around. If not, start ripping the sleeves off your shirts.
- Throw out any clothes your lady thinks make you look "cute."
- Stop sewing patches on your casual clothes. Stop sewing altogether.
- See Baker Type to Able Type, Clothing: Informal.
- Buy some flannel shirts, hooded sweat-shirts, construction boots.
- Toss all your pocket protectors, shoes by Hush Puppy, totes, earmuffs, anything velour, Bermuda shorts, and all cotton-polyester blend short sleeved button-down shirts.

Formal

- Ditch all double knits.

- See Baker Type to Able Type, Clothing: Formal. Disregard the power-dressing part; you can change, but not that much.

PERSONAL HABITS

- Never go into the bathroom again except to whiz or take a dump.
- Throw your hankies out.
- Try to grow a beard.
- Don't ask to be excused when you've finished eating.
- Learn to hawk.
- Cultivate a beer belly.
- Never write another thank-you note or Christmas card.

RELATIONS WITH WOMEN

- Move out of your mother's house. Don't get anxious—there're plenty of desperate women out there eager to clean up after you, after *anyone*.
- If a woman refuses to go out with you, call her a bitch to her face.
- Make a date, cancel, and *don't* apologize.
- Learn the difference between a linebacker and a foul line.

- Buy a bra and practice unclasping it. Don't wear it.
- Steal an ex-girlfriend's handcuffs and learn how they work.
- Don't get caught cringing in front of a woman unless it's your mother.
- When upset or angry, learn to lift your hand above your head in a threatening manner.
- Start trying to cop a feel when you're introduced to a good-looking woman.
- Stare at their tits more and cultivate a lascivious grin. A good snicker can work wonders.
- Practice lines like "How was I supposed to know?"; "What's the big deal?"; "So sue me."

RELATIONS WITH MEN

- Learn to drink Scotch neat without choking. Stop drinking anything with fruit in it.
- Practice creative swearing—"Your mother sucks bat shit off cave walls, you motherfucking, cocksucking dick licker."
- Since some of you are used to pain, you should have no problem learning to slug

and be slugged on the arm when you meet another Able type. <u>Note:</u> High fives are used when you're all pumped up because your team just scored the go-ahead touchdown. Regular fives, on the other hand, are used when someone has done something cool, like put it to some stuck-up broad who was askin' for it.

- Quit tittering and learn to guffaw.
- Smoke a cigar without coughing. Or develop a taste for nonfilter cigarettes.
- Talk about tits and ass. Learn ten synonyms for *vagina* and *labia*.
- Subscribe to a skin magazine.

OCCUPATION

- Trade in your pencils for monkey wrenches and shovels.
- Take lots of breaks and complain about the work.
- Join a union.
- Go on strike.
- Beat up a scab.
- If you have a white-collar job, learn to grab women's asses in the elevator, to base your secretary's bonus on sexual favors, and to call all women "girls."

HOME LIFE

- Throw your dirty clothes all around the house.
- Refuse to help around the house, but make sure you have a bat or a stick to defend yourself with.
- If you don't have a girlfriend, get your mom in to clean up (she will, because she's the one who made you a Charlie type to begin with).
- Mix lights and darks in the laundry.
- Go on—stick a fork in the toaster.
- Make a tower out of the cans from all the beer you've consumed in one sitting.
- Fall asleep during a football game and burn a cigarette hole in your couch.
- Stay out all night.

GENERAL ATTITUDE

- Be aggressive.
- Be hostile.
- Be slow-witted.
- Be tough.
- Be uncaring.
- Be stupid.
- Be a guy's guy.

CHANGING FROM CHARLIE TO BAKER

This metamorphosis is much simpler than the Charlie to Able change, as there are commonalities. For example, most sensitive Baker types aren't very physical because of the fear of being labeled homosexual. Able types, on the other hand, don't give a shit what people think unless you call them a faggot to their face, in which case, they'll beat the shit out of you—even if you're right. This behavior is anathema to the Charlie type.

Charlie types who want to become Baker types are usually taller than five feet seven inches. Anything shorter isn't taken seriously. Luckily they don't have to be strong, just sincere. Finally, to become an effective Baker type, the Charlie type must stop feeling sorry for himself and start feeling inadequate where women are concerned, but not concerned enough to forsake women altogether and go fag. Follow the points below.

CLOTHING

Informal

- Purchase your first set of play clothes. Anything from Land's End, L.L. Bean, or J. Crew will do.
- Lighten up the colors and maybe your attitude will follow. (Most Charlie types color-coordinate their clothes to match their bruises.) Avoid colors with pretty names.

Formal

- Keep the suits you already own, but pick up some brighter ties to go with them.
- Get rid of all your bow ties.
- Take the pennies out of your loafers.

PERSONAL HABITS

- Don't shave or bathe so much. Toss the Mr. Bubble.
- Stop biting your nails.
- Quit picking your nose and eating what you find.
- Retract your neck from your shoulders.
- Cross your legs at the ankles, not at the thighs.
- Don't part your hair in the middle.
- Learn to use mousse.

RELATIONS WITH WOMEN

- Don't cringe when being introduced.
- Stop thinking women are going to hit you every time you disagree with them.
- Instead of pouting every time a woman refuses to go out with you, tell her you'll try again some other time and call her a bitch under your breath.
- If you must cry, do it to demonstrate your sensitivity, not because her punch hurt.
- Stop apologizing all the time. Just apologize some of the time.

RELATIONS WITH MEN

- It's okay to put your arm around a male friend, but stop short of kissing.
- Swear more, but use the conventional terms like *damn*, *shit*, *hell*, etc. Stay away from the more creative forms of swearing like "suck moose cock"—that's reserved for the Able type.
- Join a co-ed reading group. Look forward to reading Gogol, Tolstoy, Turgenev.
- Only go to cocktail lounges. Stay away from bars and sporting clubs.

OCCUPATION

- Stop working with books or numbers and take a job that deals with people. People-who-need-people jobs, such as social work, teaching, or parole officer, are the best.
- Work for a woman—and like it.
- Don't call your secretary "girl" or "babe."

HOME LIFE

- Help around the house, but don't be so afraid of using Endust.
- Split child care with your wife: she takes the kids to the playground and you sit through the school pageant.
- Don't *ever* thank a woman for giving you a chore to do.
- Never wear an apron, except while barbecuing, in which case make sure it says something like KING OF THE CASTLE instead of I ALSO DO WINDOWS or HERS TOO.
- The only shopping you should be doing is for the alcohol.
- Stop drinking any alcoholic beverages that require a blender; switch from Seagram's wine coolers to Molson or Labatt.

GENERAL ATTITUDE

- Be opinionated but not threatening.
- Be helpful but not servile.
- Be forceful but not physically abusive.
- Be manly, but understand the woman's side.
- Be the provider, but also let her provide.
- Be tough, but gentle.
- Be aggressive, but repressive.
- Be yin.
- Be yang.
- Be schizophrenic.

CHANGING FROM ABLE OR BAKER TO CHARLIE

Who are you kidding? This category is reserved for masochists, closet homosexuals, and psychotics. This book is not for them.

CONCLUSION

It's time for the bottom line, the conclusion: criteria for the normal man so he can deal with the schemes of the desperate woman. These credos apply to all three male types.

Credo 1: All Men Are Normal*

It was Eve who picked the apple and got us kicked out of the Garden of Eden, yet women are always blaming men for their screwups. Don't let them fool you. You're the normal one, and don't you forget it. There's a reason our society is male-dominated, and we've got a stake to protect.

---

* Except homosexuals, silly.

Credo 2: All Women Are Desperate

No matter the type, every woman I've spoken to, including during my undercover work, wants to settle down. Many pretend they want careers, but the bottom line is that what they want is the pitter-patter of little feet. And movies, the one true barometer for the new generation, bear this out. *Baby Boom*, for example, showed us a schizophrenic Diane Keaton trying to juggle a new business enterprise and age-old maternal instincts. Guess which wins? And as these women get older, they get more desperate. How many times has your life passed in front of your eyes because you made the mistake of uttering the term *biological clock* to a single woman thirty years old or older?

Unfortunately for us, they want to get married first, and that's where the troubles start.

Credo 3: Desperate Women Are Experts at Covert Behavior

Women can talk rings around most men, which creates high levels of anxiety and frustration. This behavior can lead to the most primeval reactions, like when an Able type clocks his girlfriend upside the head for confusing him, or a Charlie type bends all his wife's grandmother's monogrammed silver teaspoons out of frustration. When a Baker type makes the error of thinking he can compete on this verbal level, he gets blown out of the water. To make matters worse, he thinks he actually won the argument.

<u>Note</u>: You must be careful. Most male arguments are rather straightforward:

MALE #1: Oh, yeah? Fuck you.
MALE #2: Well, fuck you, too.

Or:

MALE #1: Hey! You got a problem?
MALE #2: Yeah, I got a problem.
MALE #1: So what's your problem?
MALE #2: Wouldn't you like to know?
MALE #1: Oh, yeah, your momma.
MALE #2: No, *your* momma.

Etc., etc. On the other hand, women rely on nuance, inflection, and selective emphasis:

FEMALE #1: I really *loved* the way you were able to *salvage* that dinner last evening.

FEMALE #2: It was *nothing*. I cooked it that way purposely, because I've been *told* you *only* enjoy cuisines you can *spell*. You know, like "hot dogs" or "pizza."

Translation: Female #1: "Darling, fuck you"; Female #2: "Fuck you, too, honey."

Credo 4: Desperate Women Need To Change Normal Men—Immediately

These women don't have time to compromise. Instead of looking for a common ground, they'll create it, the same way a little sanitary landfill can turn a useless swamp into prime real estate practically overnight.

Note: As mentioned earlier, while we guys are paying attention during that all important first date—"Wow! Nice tits. I wonder if I can get her to stay over at my place tonight"—the woman is checking out the big picture—"Hmmm, nice arms. I bet they'd be perfect for maneuvering a stroller weighed down with our beautiful child and a bag of lawn-care products from Sears." Never forget this.

Credo 5: Normal Men Can Be Changed If They Don't Watch Out

All three types are vulnerable—after all, their mothers had at least seventeen years in which to work them over. Through the use of hidden agendas, verbal barrage, emotional nuances, sheer determination, and tears—lots of tears—women are capable of changing *any* man. The solution is to arm yourself with that terrifying fact. Use that information to protect yourself, always.

How? Sorry, I don't have the slightest idea. Maybe, once I've finished researching my next book, *The Only Thing That Separates a Normal Man From an Abnormal Man Is A, B —See?* I'll have some of the particulars worked out.

Credo 6: Misery Loves Company

You're fine the way you are. Once you understand that and see you're not the only one out there who has to deal with these desperate women, you'll feel better about yourself. You'll also see your fellow man in a different light. There's a 33-percent chance that the guy sitting or standing next to you is the same type as you. Isn't that comforting? Now, get off your butt and make that woman of yours change, for a change, or ditch her and find one who will.

Credo 7: Normal Men Must Learn to Identify the Various Female Types

As with Credo 6, if you can identify a problem, you can deal with it. When you meet a woman, take a minute to assess which type you're dealing with so you can deal accordingly. "How can I tell which type I'm dealing with?" you ask. First, reread Part II, stupid. You're not paying attention. Second, don't involve your dick in this decision-making process—it has its own agenda. Third, ask a simple question and listen carefully to the answer. For example, you might ask, "So, hey, want to go see a movie?" Alpha type might respond, "Why a movie? Can't afford tickets to the boat show?" Beta type would say something like, "Oh . . . a movie. Fine. In fact there's one playing next door to the new boat show. Oh darn, we won't have time to do both, so I guess the decision is made. Say, why don't I pick up the tickets to the boat show and you can pay me back." Finally, the response of a Gamma type would be something like, "Oh, whatever you want. I hear the boat show's nice, but what do I know?"* Third, once you've established her type . . . wait a minute. Who am I kidding? It doesn't matter which type the woman is, they're all out for the same thing: to get a man, to change him, and to make him do her bidding. I guess the only advice that really counts is watch your back.

Credo 8: Normal Men Can Change Their Types

Why bother? Take my word for it, you're going to have enough problems identifying your own type and that of your girlfriend/

* Don't be fooled by the fawning obsequiousness of the Gamma type. She's as helpless as a king cobra. I can't stress this point enough.

wife/next date. But, hey, if you simply can't bear the type God gave you, be my guest and give it your best shot. (See Part IV.) Otherwise, as Rambo would say, "Let it go."

Credo 9: "I'm Not a Misogynist, You're a Male-Directed Misanthrope."

One little "Sorry, dear, I don't agree with you," or "Fuck you, bitch, what do you know?" and we're labeled misogynists or women-haters. Well, it's our turn with the labels. Instead of getting defensive, we should practice what men do best: blind aggression. The tried-and-true no-I'm-not-you-are ploy can be pretty successful.

Alas, I can't find a single word equivalent for *men-haters*. The closest I can come is *misanthrope*, which means "a person who hates or distrusts mankind." Since it's a bit too general, tag on an appropriate modifier. So next time a woman calls you a misogynist, stare her straight in the eye and yell, "I'm not a misogynist, you're a male-directed misanthrope." Okay, I admit it's not very catchy and I can understand if you'd rather settle for something a little less clumsy, like "asshole," but it's the best the *American Heritage Dictionary* could come up with.*

Credo 10: All Self-Help Books Suck

All self-help books do is mess up perfectly good relationships. They're like having your mother-in-law or your girlfriend's best friend, the ugly, butch one who doesn't have a boyfriend and never will, sitting on your bookshelf or gazing up at you from her bedside table, a constant reminder of how awful men are in general and you are in particular.

Men, it's time to hold our heads up high and tell the women in our life that they don't have us to push around any longer. We are the new men of the next generation! (This

* If you have a better zippy phrase, or more preferably, a single word which expresses hatred of the male of the species, please send it to me care of St. Martin's Press, 175 Fifth Avenue, New York, New York 10010. I'll be pleased to help spread it around to our fellow men. Don't expect a royalty.

is where the National Anthem or "The Stars and Stripes Forever" comes in softly, gradually building to a mighty fanfare of brass and percussion.) We are the builders of great cities, the discoverers of new lands, and the architects of the future. WE ARE THE NORMAL MEN AND WE SHALL OVERCOME!!

TESTS, QUIZZES, INTERROGATIONS, EXAMINATIONS, AND PROBES

TEST #1: YOUR DEGREE OF MANLINESS

The multiple choice test below will give you some insight as to your correct type and degree of manliness. Take your time. Relax. The object is not to get them all correct. Frankly, if you do score 100 percent, you're either spending too much time studying trivia when you should be out chasing skirts, or possibly women just don't interest you. Catch my drift? If for some bizarre reason you score 50 percent or better, just rip these pages out and don't mention the results to anybody. Better yet, use a pencil so you can erase any correct answers. Good luck!

1) What does the Greek word *gonorrhea* mean?
   a) A boat powered by an Italian with a long pole (stick, not penis) around the canals of Venice.
   b) A flow of seed.
   c) Gone to Rio.

2) What is a *merkin*?
   a) A small wizard.
   b) A deep-water fish with a long nose.
   c) A pubic wig.

3) In 1492, Columbus discovered America. What else did he discover?
   a) Pizza.
   b) Syphilis.
   c) Ohio.

4) What is a Dutch cap?
   a) A funny-looking hat.
   b) A tulip protector.
   c) A diaphragm.

5) What is a "gossamer against infection, steel against love"?
   a) An iron butterfly.

b) A condom.

c) A tube of K-Y jelly.

6) Who was Richard Cornish?

a) Inventor of the Cornish hen.

b) Creator of a tasty vegetable dish called
succotash.

c) The first convicted homosexual in
America (circa 1624).

7) If you run into an ancient Egyptian male
with shaved eyebrows, what should you
say?

a) "My pyramid or yours?"

b) "Gee, sorry your cat's dead."

c) "Don't tell me—you still can't work
that electric razor."

8) What do you call a male nymphoman-
iac?

a) A nympho-woman-iac.

b) Horny.

c) A satyr.

9) What happens to a male praying mantis
after he mates?

a) She eats him—*all* of him.

b) He lights up a cigarette.
c) He promises to call her the next day.

10) What is a codpiece?
   a) Some female fish-ass.
   b) A cape off Massachusetts.
   c) Something like a jock strap you wear over your pants that makes your dick look huge.

Answers: 1)b, 2)c, 3)b, 4)c, 5)b, 6)c, 7)b, 8)c, 9)a, 10)c

Scoring: As long as you didn't answer *c* for questions (5) and (6) and *a* for questions (7) and (9), you're safe.

TEST #2: THE ENOUGH-ABOUT-THEM-LET'S-TALK-ABOUT-ME TEST

These next two quick quizzes are designed to reveal your true inner nature. Are you more romantic, or do you tend toward the practical? Do you prefer sharing a bottle of Chablis with your paramour in front of a roaring fire at some out-of-the-way country inn, or would you rather take your girlfriend to a New Jersey Devils hockey game because your boss dropped a couple of extra tickets? Complete the questions below and find out where you stand.

The Romantic You

Pick the pair of words below that comes closest to completing the analogy.

1) FRUGAL : PARSIMONIOUS ::
   a) kindly : benevolent
   b) magnanimous : philanthropic
   c) generous : prodigal
   d) stingy : miserly
   e) placid : active

2) LEOPARD : CARNIVOROUS ::
   a) tiger : striped
   b) cat : feline
   c) cow : herbivorous
   d) seal : trained
   e) quadruped : four-legged

3) CALLOW : MATURITY ::
   a) incipient : fruition
   b) spoiled : purity
   c) young : old
   d) eager : anxiety
   e) young : senility

4) SOLDIER : CARBINE ::
   a) author : book
   b) chemist : test tube
   c) sailor : pirate
   d) sailor : marine
   e) knight : lance

5) HALCYON : MARTIAL ::
   a) moon : Mars
   b) military song : warlike
   c) peaceful : warlike
   d) soothed : worried
   e) belligerent : fighting

Answers: 1)c, 2)c, 3)a, 4)e, 5)c

Results of The Romantic You Quiz
Score of 5: You don't have time to be with a woman because you're too busy in the library. Face it, you're a bore.

3–4: You don't use a condom because it "ruins the sensation and makes the love act more sterile and less personal." You also think "the whole AIDS thing is overblown," and the last time you weighed seventy-five pounds was in the fifth grade.

1–2: You can't distinguish between blush and rosé wines.

0: You don't know what the word *analogy* means.

The Practical You

Select the correct answer.

1) The product of 650 and .042 is:
   a) 273
   b) 2,730
   c) 2.73
   d) 27,300
   e) None of the above

2) 112½% of what number is 216?
   a) 182.8
   b) 243

c) 270
d) 192
e) 252

3) The number of gallons in 50 pints is:
a) 12½
b) 6¼
c) 12¼
d) 6½
e) got me

4) A woman weighs 52 kilograms. In pounds, this is about:
a) 110
b) 108
c) 114
d) 120
e) 125

5) There are n integers in the solution set of $x(x-2)(x+3)(x+5) < 0$. n equals:
a) 2
b) 6
c) 4
d) 3
e) Give me a fuckin' break!

Answers: 1)e, 2)d, 3)b, 4)c, 5)a

Score of 5: A hot date for you is bringing her to an H&R Block tax seminar.

3–4: You'd rather take your lady on mass transit than waste money on a cab.

1–2: There exists a direct proportion to how much you spend on a date and how much you expect her to put out.

0: You don't give a damn, because you're a lover not a banker.

TERMS (PSYCHOBABBLE)

We men are constantly being bombarded with psychobabble that is totally foreign to most of us, with the possible exception of a few sensitive, overeducated Baker types. Unfortunately many of these terms have become integral to the common parlance. (That means everybody's using them.) So you can stop feeling foolish or ignorant, here are definitions of the twenty most popular such psychological terms. Let's face it, it's not going to hurt to try to figure out what all those desperate women see in this "feelings" and "emotions" crap. Take your time and commit these words to memory so you can hold your own with the best of them.

1) Addiction: the opposite of subtraction.
2) Bonding: goes with *stocking*, as in "stocking and bonding"; the polite way to tie someone up.
3) Co-alcoholic: a drinking buddy.
4) Compulsive behavior: something weird you do over and over again.
5) Denial: I don't know.
6) Dependency: Polish for "depend."
7) Depression: a pothole.
8) Dysfunctional: the opposite of datfunctional.
9) Frigidity: a very cold erogenous zone.
10) Game playing: I don't know. I guess it has something to do with cards, chess, Monopoly, stuff like that.
11) Impotent: a distinguished black person.
12) Infidelity: lousy-sounding stereo speakers.
13) Intimacy: the sexual act between two homosexuals.

14) Life patterns: something you see when under the influence of LSD.
15) Manipulation: something women do to men.
16) Masturbator: a professional fisherman who's not grossed out by worms.
17) Passive-aggressive: an Italian pasta dish.
18) Schizophrenic: my mothers.
19) Subliminal cues: inferior pool sticks.
20) Vulnerability: a superhero on Saturday morning television.

PROBE: PUTTING THOSE FEELINGS INTO WORDS

List the ten most significant women in your life. Using the list of words below, write down the word or words that comes closest to describing that special woman at 1) the beginning of the relationship, 2) toward the middle of the relationship, and 3) near its end. Be sure to include the woman you're currently involved with.

angry	arctoid	anicular
amanuensis	atremia	anteambulo

amazia	barmbrack	batata
bandicoot	complicated	complaining
crawthumper	daffle	duddyfunk
ergate	figulate (adj.)	fefnicute
fizgig	fubsy	fucate
fustilugs	furtive	furuncle
guarded	heliolater	lookum
moody	misopedia	numps
outrooper	rixatrix	sinister
secretive	stirabout	tattogey
thingus	vain	wallydrag
zorillo		

I'm not sure what this little exercise accomplished, other than demonstrating how consistent you are—right? And what's wrong with that? At least you'll know what to expect in the future.

Note: For those of you with limited vocabularies, some definitions follow:

angry = mad
complaining = grumble
complicated = complex
furtive = stealthy
guarded = watchful
moody = gloomy
secretive = not frank

sinister = ominous
vain = nugatory

Oh, come on now! Don't you people know anything? Here are some more definitions:

amanuensis = a secretary who takes dictation
amazia = the absence of breasts dating back to one's birth
anicular = feeble-minded
anteambulo = an usher
arctoid = resembling a bear
atremia = a hysterical condition in which the victim cannot stand up straight
bandicoot = a foot-long rat with feet like a pig
barmbrack = a currant bun
batata = sweet potato
crawthumper = a religious fanatic
daffle = a mop used to clean an oven
duddyfunk = a meat pie found in New England
ergate = a worker ant
fefnicute = a sneak
figulate = made out of clay
fizgig = a woman who flirts
fubsy = short and plump

fucate = beautified as with paint, i.e., disguised, falsified

furuncle = a small skin boil

fustilugs = a grubby slob

heliolater = a sun worshipper

lookum = an equipment shed

misopedia = hatred of children, especially your own

numps = a twit

outrooper = an auctioneer

rixatrix = a noisy old hag

stirabout = a porridge of corn meal or oatmeal

thingus = a nobleman or knight

wallydrag = the runt of the litter

zorillo = a skunk